Maria Jastrzębska

Twenty five

For the 63 days of the Warsaw Uprisin[g] field post delivering thousands of letters [of 25] words each. Perhaps some were love lette[rs.] ..n the occasion of 25 years with my partner. I have howeve[r ...n t]ne constraint of 25 words per letter and written 25 words per stanza – 25 stanzas in all – by way of tribute. The poem draws on my own life, someone who grew up in peacetime.

How careful
you have to be,
counting each word.
Are you safe? I kiss
the nape of your neck,
kiss each finger.
Wait for me!

Were the birds
this morning
real? Lightning struck.
Rain scattered
metallic shots. I turned over
to look for you. It's the first
thing I do.

When I couldn't sleep
as a child, I'd conjure
butterflies or multi-coloured
balls bouncing instead
of severed heads
while stone-eyed executioners
closed in around me.

Remember our first
walk under the cliffs?

I lent you my jacket,
pulling it close
over your shoulders.
You wore the wrong
shoes, slip-ons, flimsy

as orange and red
butterflies, perched
on your feet.
Clouds ignited, copper
over our heads. I had no idea
the future had already
netted us.

Red's the colour
hummingbirds prefer,
they lick nectar
with their forked tongues
from red flowers more than
any others. *Bei mir
bistu shein,* sweet red.

What did we laugh about?
Laugh about now?
I don't know. We snicker
sudden as horses,
bolting, kicking, bumping.
Jaws loose, nostrils
soft and round.

On the dance floor
everyone wants a turn
with you. You hop,
shim sham, slide.
I lead, attempt to,
you follow –
we both know.

6

Remember the man
at your mum's wake
whose coat caught
on fire, the woman
at my mum's who asked
which business
we were partners in?

On the beach
men tell me stories.
At the buoy. Exhausted.
Panic attack. Treading
water, I thought
of my daughter.
You give me that look.

When we quarrel
I lie awake, then your hand
creeps across all those
frozen rivers, outwitting
scavengers between
drops of rock
and ice, finds mine.

Words are ants
carrying moments.
I want each one
to count. But illness
rattles the window –
a past lover, disgruntled.
Some days are just lost.

Fi got caught
kissing another girl
in the school library.
We thought it was funny
then her parents
and the family doctor
had her sectioned.

7

Maeve said she
couldn't chance
upsetting her husband,
not when he was being
really good about everything,
because if he decided
to go for custody

he'd win,
no doubt about it,
and if she lost
her little girl,
her scamp, her *stór*, if that
happened she'd surely
lose her mind.

You didn't know
those women –
or Shireen and Pat
knocked off a park bench
trampled into grass.
Who will remember
their lives, our good luck,

marches, tea-dances,
your cakes, the parties,
bonfires, wigs, outlaw
moustaches? Tonight
I undo your dress where
that button is stiff.
You say you always dream

you can't find
your shoes. Darling,
if I could, instead of
crumbs or pebbles,
everywhere you went,
I'd leave a shiny
pair out for you.

Not *'our'*, just our
children clamber on.
From under the duvet
we make a volcano
with our knees.
It erupts to throw
them off squealing.

Then the dead decide
to muscle in.
No room! I explain.
In lamé, pink thigh-length
boots, M&S cardigans,
uniforms, insist on settling
in our silence.

Almost forgot –
cats. The bat which flew in,
tomatoes you planted
tangled by storms.
Everyone we love.
Swims, hill walks
with a brother. Are we

old? You call yourself
my pile of washing,
I answer I'm your
bundle of sticks.
Who cares? If I
gather you up,
you collect me.

You edit better.
Ocean views, hotel
linen, bougainvillea,
le Marais, trains, snow ?
I'd keep it all. Need
a loft. Lots of lofts.

Lofts of lots.
Red, blue, green,
yellow. From the kitchen
I see the string of lights
you hung round
our spindly fig tree.
Night suns
colouring my dark.

Wait! Endings arrive
too soon. I need
twenty-five more
years at least, still have
so much to tell you!
Kissing your fingers
one by one.

Simon Perchik

Five Poems

*

It's how this hillside weeps —a rain
any minute now will cover the stones
each mourner leaves to help you find

the way back —you dead are always thirsty
and though there is no shore you drift
as the last breath to leave its hiding place

—it's a cemetery! why are you belting out
one love song after another as if no one
can hear you reaching into the Earth

with a voice worn down to the bone
by lips that no longer move
are used to making it home in the cold

sent to bed as snow —before and after
covered with footsteps louder and louder
giving up everything just to cry.

*

Always for the first time this bathroom mirror
begins its life as a windshield, not yet bent
from leaning down for mist and a better look

becomes the only instrument you can trust
—to your face shows where the sky once was
and with the same silence reaches up

is over and over washing your hands
watching them fall as rain or no rain
though the glass you can't see through

is in pieces one by one filling each faucet
with engine sounds from this small sink
as if nothing now will close or let go.

*

Where the window ends a naked mannequin
looks over her shoulder as if she feels your hand
keeping warm on her breast while the captain

stands guard at the bow —she's waiting for the dress
to unfold full-sail, pull at the damp sleeves
till her arms reach around the sun and knot

keeping still the waves from that first sea on Earth
—to this day all cloth is filled with enchantment
—tailors learn this early, use a single thread

trickling from some department store to hold fast
moving you closer to her —you become the shallows
have no other place to go now that the shore has dried.

*

You kiss the way every headstone
takes its first breath from some mountain's side
and never lets go, is washing over you

as the distance that empties the Earth
by pointing overhead and all night
pours into your mouth the cry

no longer breathing out —your grave
is making way for another, waiting for the sky
to come closer, no longer in a circle

lay side by side the way all shadows
now face the afternoon, once as silence
and now in the open, has your warmth.

*

This mannequin is used to miracles, a new jacket
warming where a breath should be —the dead
know all about how a window ices over

where there was none before, kept lit
for the floodlights to break open the glass
—you're still bleeding and the police

will ask for your name though the small stone
was made whole piece by piece by holding you
the way each corner moves closer to another

—there's a word for this and you are here
to give it life, shop from a grave
that is not a bomb to break open

and for a few minutes there's the long ago
shattered, the breathing faster and faster
as your name, over. over and over while it lasts.

Tomi Adegbayibi

On Cobalt Roads the Trees Are Ultramarine

The way home is not lost, is not hidden or potholed. Its floors are paved with ores seeping crystalline Atlantic drying cobalt glass. The glass is road, is path, is forever. The air above forever is always wind, always salt of oceans. The way home is not void, is not pigmented abyss is iris   Irises ashen ing piles of sand trapped between green and purple. Trees feathered peacocks. Children of women of men hiding behind the bodies of feather   trunks seeking their roots.

A woman born along this road grills plantains and yams for no one. Halfway south, halfway self – hyphenated heritage. The way home is a lazuli bunting's song trapped in the stomach of a boy-man learning Lingala, Lapis glass winding in on itself.

Part way north a group with mouths filled with hydrangeas walk in the direction of their grandparents, in the direction of their grandchildren, an always of backs bending forward and back.

There is laughter and exile. There is a girl reading Soyinka into a hole in a tree. It swallows her and the Mediterranean. Reads plays and poems to the ocean floor.

The way home is dispersed. Scattered webs of saxe silk.

Suspended in space, a stretch of road that is there and that is here.

Walking has removed its feet.

An open road, its new trees, its body of leaves, of veins and sky.

Returning.

Retreating.

For the Drillers on Obsidian Streets

Black is black on its own / Human the weight inside shadow
/ No one begs for hunger / And hunger eats the traces of
light that light the path / Till it's right we'll do wrong / From
the bodies spill juice turned felsic lava / Harden the streets
obsidian / And the ones still alive are speaking / Between the
bars the beats they're bleeding / The songs wrong until they're
right / Boys boys until they're men / A system crumbling
until it's dead / Some snow / Some Ice / Took some to die /
Some shadow / Some glass / When we do wake up / We try
/ Some art / Some drill / It's dark until its light.

Oolong

Tress planted without seeds, heritage in bark, in leaf.
The infant grows safest in high altitudes,
far from the world, far from abuse...

...the mist to shield, the farmer protects growth and taste.
Maturity complex, innocence preserved.
Notes of honeysuckle and air...

Orange Music Room

Some people open their mouths and make blue a plural to itself. Voice to texture. Vibrato. I try to makes myself believe these words are music enough, turn the blues into the lighter shades of purple I feel, turn sibilance into soft falsettos.

I am sitting in Nina's orange room. She's singing of Mississippi and Baltimore. No one wipes the sweat from her brow. Tony Allen peels a tangerine made from the skin of his drums, all the songs of Fela leaking out. As it pours, we step over colonial corpses. Coltrane and Miles run scales between each other till they are tired, till the scales too are tired and the walls shed. Nina mourns her walls, mourns female, mourns black.

The room, is a chamber of echoes running forward, moving ears, and throats. My ears. My throat. I am in a room of before trying to make sense of now. The pen useless. The sounds, the walls, their voices solid citrus mist.

Some people open their palms, squeeze their fingers, make synonyms of sounds the spaces between words could not utter.

Fran Lock

Poem in which i became a bear

and fled to the sawtoothed haunts
of the forest, distended and gestating.
the bear had been swelling inside
of me – a cervical cyst with a thicket
of hair – since ninety-eight. *unkindly
form*, unkempt and eager-eyed. all
her stares were sidelong. bear would
be born, a stiff aura of fur, radiating
outwards like a halo from my cunt.
sundered, surrendered, not knowing
how to say. so *bear.* you could drown
in bear, all your precious memories
accessible to fire. bear would be
worn on the outside. not your soft
bear: stuffed animal eyes turned
to the wall. no, not a *stuffed bear*,
but a girl *stuffed* with being bear.
this crypt of thistles. hair-quake,
hair-waltz, a carny's horny bearded
bride. a bear is a threshold. a bear
is a fur terminus. carnivoran
frontier, self-lubricating howl.
in the forest i licked my shame
to shape. there were tremors
there was vomit. until i became
upholstered in bear, until i became
a sprinting crouch, bellowing my
bleak disclaimers to the hills:
come at me! i dare you! my mouth
grew long, innovating bayonets;
i gathered mass. pick the crust
off a girl, there's a bear beneath.
he thinks he did this. they think

i think he did this. they think
i am sorry. a bear is a stain becomes
part of the design. i have eaten men
alive, corrupted and replete,
i have hugged my own consoling
bulk all night long. between
maiden and *mother*, a bear. her
shape stirred into the circumpolar
sky like nuts in fucking yoghurt.
not a skybear, i. no azimuth. no
altitude. no *catalogue of stars*.
i choose the damp earth under
me, close enough to him to
take off his head.

Iphigenia

stapled eyelids, steepled fingers, *sleep*.
my telescope has sleuthed the swarming
stars for signs. by *telescope* i mean my
eye. my eye is a torchbearer, rearing
its manifold fires. my fires, leaping in
relays. there's a light inside of men, both
permanent and obsolete. this moon has
bitter marvels; banalities and guises,
throes. some monster stalks my
ornamental histories, sluggish scent
of vervain, silver cimaruta, all my
apotropaic charms. staunch and bane.
my ruing herbs. and i would sleep,
succumb to its eddying medicine. but
sleep is a false friend, and plenty enough
of that when i'm – stare into the riddling
abyss of self-absorption; the mirror
turns my calculations jagged, my saffron
robes to rope. i come at myself
obliquely in a semi-circular motion;

my eyebags are crowded with cotton
balls. a girl is a kind of professional
orchid. my veil becomes oblivion;
i practice myself through a fine
tulle mesh. oh girling fate, textbook
of transparencies. *maiden*
is a codliver word mutating
in a liturgical spoon. i know what's
coming. father on the stairs, creaking
to correct my gravity. he's prepared
the pyre, a paraffin digression
among the heaped briquettes.
a *big man now*, all his principals
distilled to oath inside a smoky
glass. a bad day concentrate
in a chipped tooth, in a nicked
chin, in tiny tissue paper squares.
his uniform, buttoned to comeuppance,
and up he comes. something shiny
and primitive is polishing itself along
the edge of my presentiment. his eyes
are running like undercooked egg. he
has muck on his boots; he bears the green
dirt like a perfume, has kicked
the malfunctioning flora into heaps.
there's a knot tied in his tight, white
binding. my spine is a ribbon for
stringing beads. here is the night's
girdling hand. my thighs move into
alignment. he says my name. my name
becomes a blush becomes a stutter,
tunnel to redundancy.

My life as a popular frieze

i had my cults and carvings,
xoanon and effigies, small
wonders worked in wood.
i laid the path. i made
the mark. from ipecac,
a rhizome dried, i drew
the dark. set spinning
sun and moon. this world
was never yours, you
softboiled boys. but now
my sheeted icons stare
from cat-piss peeling corners.
and the room is bare. listen:
egged on and three-sheets
on shore leave, peleus liked
a sickle place in me;
my filaments and lamellae.
my fertile surface. fruiting
body firm. these gills, these
scales, more lachrymose
mouths. *cry all you want,*
decanting the day's quota
of honeyed doom into
the shape of me. i had my
acolytes, my aspects, all
my subtle ways of raving.
his damask, anaglypta,
chintz, a theory of hysteria.
wandering womb, my
chambered brain was
wayward. honeycomb's
compressive strength,
my suspect structures
riddled from within. i
was a snake, was a lion
in a fire, and a strong wind

wheeling his ship
toward the rocks.
his was an abductor's
grip. proficient finger,
crooked to fishook pun.
caught, *landed*, gaping.
would strip entreaty
out of air. had i breath.
the taste of his flesh
burns brackish. i
am a razor shell, pried
apart. i had my rites
and prophesies: in
nine months time
they'll hang me at
the end of the jetty
like a shark, slit
my belly and see
what falls out –
a licence plate
a glass amphora
a mostly mortal child.

I am told

that dry land is not a myth. i am told there are women
who come with the neatness of an undertaker's sneeze.
i am told about myself. by poets, mainly. in the freeze-
dried stickling of their lauded forms. days of equivocal
spleen, dear god. today i am sick, itching, slick with my
obsessions. i have learnt eruption from the gulls. a way
to make my whiteness mob. my body sings its curvature
of dirt, its cells, is pasty and assailable. i am told to
speak up, to voice all the unsaid sinews of this hurt,
the heart one cartoon bicep flexing. one big rubber
muscle. i am told we can live on thirty pounds a week,
what to do if my symptoms persist, of my imploded

promise first. *alms for the poor,* and how i let him
down. a girl is dicking around, mudlark at the limits
of the criminal. i hate the cocaine cosiness of her to
death. smugly wayward. one day, diva, you'll be barefoot
backstage, fixing your own hair. you'll be mariah carey
advertising fucking crisps. hyena will not wait for
the law to have mercy, nor to be adored. i am told an
animal cannot suffer. hyena is the suffering tongue,
stuck out. her dead name. her deadly name, i mean.
love, conditioned and conditional. the pigs in their dalek
glide behind farmfoods, steady rain, and kfc, with its ugly
confederate albinism. the stink from extractors, all
day long. lips meeting with a voluptuary shush. i am
told about love in its low-hanging dopamine: tedious.
hyena, annulling a nervous blush by opening
a vein, by picturing the key, confirming the prison.
which is literal and everywhere, by the way. her
desire is a double negative. bare with promise. i am
told how brave, in spirals of grimacing ecstasy,
a guardian interview leaking its feels. oh please,
enough. i am going spare. i mean. is a poem ever
more than a high-pitched whine about legal violence?
ticking of the endometronome. a skew-eyed pain
out of sequence. fuck. i am told it gets better. i am
told to take up yoga. i am told to live what
i fucking love.

Stuart Cooke

The Space Between

What the dusk has done
is let mist settle on the valley;
dark ridges protrude, like the spines
of ancient sea creatures, from its woollen veil.

The sky's still blue enough, but it's burning up
along the border with the earth, most of which is obscured
by the blackest ridge, slumped across the foreground,
insisting that everything follow it into night
(you can't see its details anymore,
other than the cauliflower silhouettes of a few trees along the saddle
and its fierce gradient, sloping
into the centre of the scene,

but just a moment ago, across the valley
where there aren't any roads,
I saw a single light
travelling down the shoulder, flittering
between murky wads of bush,
and it seemed like life was beginning to weave
into dream, when,
at the very instant the light vanished,
my eyes were caught by a single bird—darkened,
distant, perhaps a kestrel—
gliding through black space and the woollen valley
and the embers beneath the sky,
and you were there with me, or you could have been,
before you were gone).

Cicadas

1.
At first it's wave-after-
wave of music surging forward, welling
into a gigantic monument of rush,
into great, crashing heaps of click-cracks—
suddenly receding, only for a moment,
now building again, into a heaving, sonic bulldozer,
dominating space, annihilating it, as your ears throb like gourds
on either side of your head.

The apple gums seem entranced.
Really, there's nothing but this music, its throb landscape,
its Australianness;
it streams through crevices and crannies, fills fields
until we're weightless in its ocean.

The campers can't hear each other;
the men at the pub let it fill the gaps in their conversations
and overflow until it speaks, better than any language of ours,
of the force beneath the present, of its clarity, how it bubbles and stretches,
how it cools and sets at night.

When the waves recede, thoughts return.

2.
Surely, after thunder and machinery, this is the continent's loudest sound.
Meanwhile, the dim forests of the Americas
are dominated by the howler monkey's bellow: miniature ape,
loudest mammal, he draws his territory with a cyclone.

But a smaller continent demands a smaller cry,
a shrunken monkey, an Australian insect; if the sound
of the Americas is a little man's roar,
then Australian sound is composed of innumerable miniatures,
which up close might appear unremarkable, even alien,

but in tandem can surge, flooding forests and thoughts
with their invisible, impossible presence.

Gathering on the trunks of the bush, buckling and unbuckling
their tymbals to build their chorus—here it comes again,
swelling once more through the valley and across cleared country,
swallowing up cows, cars, children,
compiling that enormous opera, unstoppable until it collides
with the bricks of human settlement.

You could sit for hours, mind round as a drum.

Gareth Culshaw

Bits and Pieces of Who He Is

The chin he found in a stonewall holds sunlight
for his working hours. He grubs up another work day,
pushes the tractor wheels out of a gate.
Rooks fetch back the blackness he hides in his head,
as they stagger across the ploughed sky,
bend the rawky air with their caw.
There's signs of orange peel in his fingernails,
but he never eats on the whim of a hedgerow.
He catches his face in a rose petal when the morning
rises from the nest of night.
The thought of oak branches, shape his arms,
allow him to stand against the coughing wind.

Sometimes he shears sheep in a pen. Grabbing
them by the throat, he yells into their faces.
He seems to think we're all part of his flock
as a frown escapes his whittled fringe,
when you pass him walking the dog.
The shaved wool whitens his beard fills the hair
he lost when his youth died.
He skittles the sheep with his stare whistles
the tractor homeward to unmute the silence.

Herding

I see the farmer up the tops herding cattle with cracker-snapping
knuckles. The field folds into the numbed earth makes cows
stumble their tongues with each footstep.

A gate stays open, allows a wind to escape the farmer's gapped teeth.
He bows a spine too broken for an office job, shoves the arse
of a cow he's supported through nail-clipping rain.

His tractor sits in the corner as the tyres hunch the metal body.
A rotovator hides within brambles lost to the spin of the sky.
Two wooden gates lean into each other, mutter in the winds.

He heaves a cloud shadow out of the field watches the cattle
stamp their hooves to another gate. His dog snaps at a frozen breath
that falls from the throats of each buckled head.

A gate is closed with a hand clenched by January. He fumbles
his body down the slope to his tractor, grinds out a rind of noise
leaves the field to hooves and slobber.

The Morning Farmer

In the shock of wind that follows his milk delivery
the farmer brings to the boil a duck egg.
Glides butter along the scree of toast, hears a kettle
stir up the morning clouds. He stands within the silence
of his house, waits for the crow to balance out
a telephone post in his garden. Pops open a mouth
for a drop of milk, feels it slide into his bark-tight body.
Out the window, summer leaves his garden via the sky,
as brambles wilt to wiry frames, and rose petals
tuile winter's cough. He pushes back his hair allows
a lemonade-sigh to climb the soil-fed skeleton.
His elbow whimpers as he tries to stretch out lost youth.
The kettle tuts, twitches his eyebrows as a bull shaking
off flies. He pours his night into an empty mug, snorts
a biscuit wrapper, plonks his body to form a sack
of himself. The wind foreplays with the letterbox brings
a draft to wake up his back. Slippery sunlight opens
up the fields spares the jackdaws its light, sheep move
to widen the earth as the farmer dunks five more minutes
into his sugar-filled tea.

He Whirs the Morning out of Bed

He catches the sunlight in his blades
as he grides the sprint of summer.
A flat cap hides away blue moonlight
that puddled his head during sleep.

The engine disturbs chaffinches who make
a dazzle for the oak. Sheep, stay far off,
keep the field's silence in their heads.
A tractor muzzles the road flicks up mud

to hide the stars. He wherrits the hedge
gives wings to a blackbird who drops
a worm. Seventeen rooks escape his brow
leave him alone to the cawing crow.

An itch forms on his forearm and he stops
the whirring to catch the legs. He spits a broken
cloud to glisten a woodlice shell. A smell
of green surrounds his overalls and a shadow
falls off him as the sun swells above the hornbeam.

Fokkina McDonnell

All advice is reversible

like the silk jackets from *Patra*, in a paisley pattern or cobalt blue. If you're slight and short, you could become a jockey, but you've probably left it too late to turn into a horse. A horse is always two halves, anyway, and refrains are the life blood of pantomime. If you want a moustache, I recommend Charlie Chaplin, rather than Adolf H. Bear in mind that Churchill also fancied himself as a painter. *Avant-garde* is fine here on the continent. I didn't know what *spotted dick* was when I arrived in little England. And I asked a man about *pouffe pastry*. I can see *you* are sophisticated already and can tell your fettucine from your philistines, your syphilis from your Sisyphus. Yes, I agree: a rolling stone gathers no moss.

Dear Darkness

I apologise sincerely for only now replying to your invitation. I have already tried to be a lighthouse, but that didn't work. Perhaps, it is because we are all orphans, and we focus on the small window. It wasn't clear to me from your earlier letter (the one you sent via Japan, after Sumiko's death). We must respect people's wishes, don't you agree? Because our piano tuner was blind and Helmut Walcha was a blind organist, I didn't want to have lessons. So sad, he became blind after being vaccinated for smallpox. I'm sorry, Darkness, I'm going off on a tangent. With travelling east several times each year, I have lost the odd hour. *For now, we see only a reflection in a mirror.* The dark of the coal shed. When I was 12 and I saw my grandmother in hospital (I was supposed to leave things with a nurse), I beckoned the quiet man in the dark suit. He is always there, walking two feet behind me, a dutiful wife. You know well enough I've been looking ever since for the ferryman's smile. Since 1977, to be precise.
Best regards,

Between France and Spain

they dared to stretch the day's measure.
Constant companions: the sun, the valleys,
small dead songbirds caught on metal wire.
For each songbird they created a song, mostly white.
They walked towards a village. Outside the butcher's
the flashing yellow outlines of a small pig.

The songs waiting in their head fizzed.
They were naughty schoolboys, slightly ashamed
that they hoped to find more dead songbirds.
Their thoughts would have been carbon dated
if that technique had been invented.
Their spittle knew nothing of DNA tests.

They counted the remaining notes.
An eruption of chords would be the title
of their composition. The evening sky
grew darker as they cleared away the knives.
They had gone down the long road,
a black measuring tape in front of them.

The word *potential* fired them, kept them
walking, counting, measuring.
Potential witness, if there was a job title
for the solid task they aimed to complete.
They were pilgrims, their pilgrimage
a resistance against amnesia.

Ultimately, everything is an act of resistance.
The black measuring tape being rolled up
while the green grass, green hills are immune,
do not know how to spell *amnesia*. We are engaged
in an experiment, they said to each other.
Chirping crickets faded. At last they were ready to sleep.

Note: *borrows a line from Kei Miller's 'Establishing the Metre'.*

Three Nocturnes

Falling asleep is like stepping into a lift

The sick moment when it falls before it rises. Or falling asleep is returning to a house you no longer own. Being asleep is the white noise of snow. But the rooms in that house are empty, and you live in a town with a foreign name. Sleeping, waking, dreaming. You may as well start on your tasks. The fullness of an unholy trinity: cold smoke, a rusting railway line to nowhere, bare feet slipping from the track. Half a moon.

The train driver

...On sick leave since the fatality and a *route refresh* needed before they allow me back to work. When I can't sleep, I run through the routes in my mind: stations, signals, tunnel entrances, slow bends, bridges where people drop rubbish on the four-foot. Give me the open space any day, like the clear run up to Penrith...

> taking an empty
> to the depot –
> moon through bare trees

How to calculate the ratio of night to nightfall

1. Allow (+/- 1.24) for *true* nocturnal.
2. Error code 400? Check for rain and clouds.
3. Adjust for seasonality (4) and continental drift.
4. Factor in wasps, using the Conway chained-arrow notation, or the Steinhaus-Moser notation.

Paul Rossiter

A Visit to Runmarö

in memory of Tomas Tranströmer

the ferry backs carefully away from the jetty
in a frothy swirl

and then the water settles

skerries   wooden jetties
the road
rises gently from foreshore to forest

  I swallow the silence-potion

pine   silver birch   rowan
a red house where a crowd of ferns
has quietly advanced all the way to the doorstep

gravel-surfaced, the road winds
through forest, marsh and meadow
past school, chapel and graveyard

and now here's the poet's name
hand-written on a green mailbox at a junction
where a modest track leads off through trees
towards a steep slope down to the stony shore

'there it is,' says the old lady walking her dog
pointing to a small two-storey house

pale blue shingle walls
windows outlined in darker blue
red-tiled roof with a red-brick chimney
all placed on a platform of patient grey boulders

a house that senses
the constellation of nails that holds its walls together

garden chairs are stacked on the porch
the house is quiet, keeps itself to itself,
behind the glass of the living room window
a dangle of wind-chimes hangs motionless
as though waiting for someone to return

I walk back through forest
past scattered houses, past meadows
past a reed-fringed lake

the earth is springy under my feet
and I suddenly understand that plants are thinking

at the jetty, half an hour to wait for the boat

The Pleasures of Peace

1

Sirens wail and steel objects fall from the sky,
giving banks and insurance offices heart attacks, axe-blow spasms
    that shrug masonry off its foundations –
building after building climbing down itself into the street to be
consumed in fire.

This happened before I was born, but as a small child,
peering through gaps in rickety wire-and-picket fencing, I saw
ruined cellars and shattered brickwork,
tattered wallpaper adorning ghost rooms two storeys up,
traces of vanished stairways climbing propped-up walls,
and lakes of rosebay willow herb – sheets of ruffled purple
mantling the rubble and bared earth of basements opened to sky.

2

When a fire or other disturbance opens up the ground, the seeds of *Chamaenerion angustifolium* germinate. Some areas can, after burning, be covered with dense stands of this species; in Britain in the 1940s the plant became known as 'bombweed' due to its rapid colonisation of the bomb craters.

3

Seventy and more years on, the trees on Hampstead Heath
heave their shoulders and rustle their spreading limbs like giants doing
     Tai Chi.
A sudden alarm call, and an unseen blackbird thrashes away through the
     heavy summer foliage.

Lifting its head above a bed of brambles, a single purple flower
stirs and sways, attentive
to the fleeting motions of the wind.

Among trees, across grass, through bracken, skirting thickets,
the path leads on like a thought.

Tour Guide

EP: *Thrones, Drafts & Fragments*

1

White-bearded, wearing his signature dark overcoat and hat, walking slowly with his stick, the poet shows me around the penultimate volume of his epic.

It isn't a book, though, it's a room: museum-like, irregularly shaped, with dim lighting, dark corners and alcoves, full of glass cases containing mummies and grave goods of extraordinary magnificence.

The poet, silent, leads me from exhibit to exhibit, occasionally pointing out a detail with his stick. The overall impression is one of incomparable splendour. But, after all's said and done, these are, of course, dead bodies.

2

After long silence, the poet at last reveals the concluding volume of his work. It isn't a book, though, it's a train: he conducts me to a seat in one of the carriages.

The journey isn't long. The track runs through suburban housing, then along a shopping street with a bank on every corner. We pass several Renaissance palazzi and glimpse across a canal a row of restored mediaeval houses painted in pristine colours.

The train enters a park whose main feature is a temple set back against – perhaps even carved out of – a rock face. It's unfinished, encased in scaffolding and swathed in protective sheets.

I then realise that the railway tracks ran out some distance before we reached this point, and the train is now immobilised, sunk to its axles in sand.

The weather's halcyon, the light clear and haunting.

There's no obvious way back.

Gerrie Fellows

from Shadow Box:
Poems from the Hunterian Museum

Object: Carved Stone Ball

403.6 grams
Locality: Aberdeenshire
3200–2500 BC

Handheld   a weighted sphere
deeply grooved to fit a fingering
the whole hand takes part in

a plaything for the mind
come to us from the past   iron-dark
speckle of biotite in granular stone
worked by Neolithic hands
in a tooled, ancient trade

The mind asks for meaning
gets a curve ball, carved   ancestrally wielded
an object willed
                but not into the unknown

Unknown is only where we find ourselves
enquirers desiring to recognise
a symbol of power
    an artefact of ceremonial
        a device for speech   memory   story

for guesswork   our best guess
for an object blessed with guesses

turning   as if in the dark

We are in the dark
the object shines in the light
        glitters with Scottish earth

Cast

of the left hand of Frederyk Chopin
Medium: bronze

Gold-knuckled in metallic skin
inhuman   scattering light

the stilled dimension
of bones, flexed tendons
the hypermobile
immobilised to a single piece

his dead hand   plastercast
in transition from being to artefact
cast from the body
to sombre bass notes

keys his living hand had spanned
string and hammers
sounding the heart's velocities

The ear, too, has a hammer
as had the craftsman who shaped
the shell of wood and air
in which the music resonates

from which all the living notes rise up
as if weightless
yet bearing the weight of grief and love

cast to the air where sound plays
on the small bones of the ear

After-Image

(Photogram for Emily Dix, 1904-1972
pioneer palaeobotanist)

In morning vapour   a trace
on the window pane of a single dragonfly
or was it a shadow that alighted here
as if among seed fern and horsetail

her findings
from the black fuel of the coalfields –
a tweed-skirted field geologist
whose inventive mind crossed the boundaries
of the Upper Carboniferous

On display
findings that survived wartime bombing
Neuropteris attenuata, Lepidodendron ophiurus

but not range charts, research notes
her thoughts
that burned bright as fern fronds in coal

No note of the frontal leucotomy
that cut through a mind
high-flying through seed fern and horsetail
Neuropteris schlehani, Annularia stellata

The image on the glass
(diffuse as a foot print in snowmelt)
unfossilised, mutable imprint
Emily Dix among the nine floral zones
of the Upper Carboniferous

Kaitaka

Rectangular cloak
in a single weave
South Island, Aotearoa New Zealand
(18th century)

flax, double-twined
ornamented with clusters of feathers
a patterned edge   encased
as if without weight against weather

there is a question of distance
a question of orientation
a border   the direction of feathers
meanings hidden or brought forward

how to understand what is seen
as a map of the past
or as a map with the tracks of birds

groundweave of tussock and flax tuft
bird calls knotted into it   kiwi feathers
        orange (as of small fires)
        night-sky blue of pukeko

a knowledge passed down in the body
        flighty   or earthbound

a question the weaver answers
netting sky and windblown earth

Carrie Etter

from The Sentences

The sentence declares it's a cold day in early March, the maple and sycamore leafless, the daffodils tawdry with yellow. Proffer or promise. There's a reckoning of days, an interminable catalog, a diminishment by number. Such small rooms know little oxygen. *Heave ho*, says the old man walking his little dog. *Heave ho.*

* * *

There's always chatter in the off license. *Let me tell you about sentences, or don't talk to me about Heidegger.* There are tins of baked beans, plastic bags of spaghetti, sixteen flavours of potato crisps. *But how cold does it feel?* The most frequently bought wines have either palm trees or sea vistas on their labels. Chuck, chuck.

* * *

If one can take a sentence for a walk, how does it work in a loop, the widely favoured form of walk: does the sentence end with the same word with which it began or somehow end just before it, so the first word could be touched with an outstretched hand? The loop goes down the road, up the slope, to the right past the green, along a further, flatter right through poplars and the occasional skitter of dogs, down further right into the turn, over a mud path that in summer is banked with blackberries and offers a view of sheep on the far hill. The sentence can cover a lot of ground. In the distance, looming, the wonderful If.

Before Elegy

Even now you love a dying creature. Okay, aging.

In one hand, the phrase: a year or two. In the other: months.

At the park you overhear, "Well, the sun'll come up tomorrow," and you're all *maybe in your fucking world*.

You try not to watch the dogs or the children in their nimble extraordinary simple.

Thankfully, winter. The long dark and the heavy wine.

If only the night's windows did not reflect your face.

Another California

A god will meet you in the desert, amid the saguaros, the lizards, a single coyote.

By god you meant mirage in a moment of extremity, right?

The dry heat amplifies your physical awareness to the fine hairs on your philtra.

You left the bottle of water in the rental car because that was the kind of journey you wanted.

Before long, a distant shimmer, a mental clarity or vacuum, every pore open.

Even here, your name clings to you, as merciless as.

Cliff Yates

The Detective's Raincoat
(after Lisa Jarnot)

Not to pretend to be snow, but to taste it, your tongue
burning with cold like a picture frame, to hear
the bicycle inside the earth as the world tumbles
like a gobstopper inside your mouth, and not to be king
for a day but to dream of oranges, gobstoppers, snow
and the radio through the wall, music and voices
from under the carpet, and to make floorboards
creak in the dark, to know where they creak
and where they don't on the silver staircase
with its fabulous promises, and not to be a prisoner
but to do without salami and pastry, to welcome
bewilderment and uncertainty and the wind over tiles,
the sound of the refrigerator when you open
the door, the muscular horses, and to spin
in the downward pull, the freedom to consciously fall.

Tonight We're Showing a Film

People no longer queue outside the cinema
in flat caps and headscarves this isn't the 1950s.
Two girls are singing in the toilets it's the acoustics.
We should rent them out as a recording studio.

We're showing *Something in the Air*
directed by Olivier Assayas. It's a good (French) film.
There's a lot of fire and dreaming.
Set in the 70s it's coolly nostalgic

the soundtrack's outstanding and everyone
is earnest mostly. The police are violent.
Well they can be, that's not fiction
and setting alight to buildings is violent.

We have problems with the lighting man.
He was up all night watching the election.
Well, who wasn't? Dreamy adolescence,
politics and art, that's not a bad combination.

Further On

In *Three Colours Blue*, she's underwater,
trying to hide from whatever's inside
behind the glass that brings her closer to us
because 'we're all behind glass in this world.'

Further on, her name's gone and not even
sugar, dissolving on the spoon, is a distraction
as through her eyes the doctor speaks,
mattress on floor, the shutters open.

And in the queue for the escalator
on New Street station, the boy
with the mohican bides his time
carrying a massive pair of wings.

Three days after the death,
a white feather. Nothing lasts forever.

Simon Smith

A Note to It

It became immediately apparent that the poem I was living in had stopped meaning. Its batteries were dead, its discourse had run its course, its markets crashed. Utilities were disconnected, the place inhospitable.

Like scattered wrappers, the writing fell silent. At rest. *In medias res.* Unidentified militias occupied. Cables cut, wires tapped, windows taped & prepped for the blast. Levers, buttons, the cursor unresponsive. Exhausted, inert, useless.

Useless as the machinery of coke furnaces, or steel mills, or metaphor. Essentially Time & Space had changed, so the language could no longer function. The dead arrived in squadrons, were already there. Trade halted. A ruin uninhabitable.

I was floating in rooms, corridors, passages – places of change & transition that were constantly changing, and then not changing at all. Then Time was blocked. In so far as I exist I am in the folds, the creases, the hinge. Suspended.

I was closer to the dead than the living. It was safer to discourse with them, to mix, conspire the Truth. There were bare wires – earth, "live," neutral. Incognito. Or at the edge. To kiss the living meant almost certain death. Statistics, stasis.

I was more alive in my dreams than waking hours & tuned to birdsong. Like a blindman from out of town. "Mayday, Mayday, Mayday". The trafficator flashes the warning, right. Autocued.

My father, who died seven years ago, came back to life. "Great to see you, dad." "Great to see you, son." We never called one another "dad" or "son". In fact, he says nothing but drives cars.

Time stopped. So, I lived by night, talked with the dead, read off the Ouija board. The corridors narrowed. I took beer, wine & whiskey. I listened to the radio at night. I became a radio. I am a radio. All night. Static. "I" am Greek & I am posthumous.

I dwell in a caravan, & Elvis is dead, but it is no longer the summer of '77, & the writing had stopped meaning, felt silent. The regiments of the death's heads. To know where to look. To know how to look, to know.

It's the ghosts that are speaking now instead, on the inside, tapping the Morse along skirting-boards. I read Spicer, listen in, glass to the wall, ear cupped. Time is stopped. "Now" is nocturnal & vibration.

This "house" means "ark". Now that the ghosts are speaking us & have moved in, I am their guests with interests in code. Now they are the ones gathering curtains into pencil pleats, pins in their mouths.

I connect to the world's silence, to snatch a signal from out of air, to drag along the zip-wire, the blood rush where vessels transport vessels, vessels people. I signify via a series of magic lantern slides.

Passage

is a message passed on from the music bureau to the hive-mind
the morning star catches the earth every five hundred & eighty-fourth day
my evening star parsed
the delicate labyrinthine of the lung
the alveoli the touch of O^2 CO^2 & blood
a universe a memory as many connections as stars
& the cry in mimicry of my Chinese whisper
tracking where the morning crosses stirs wavelengths
transmitter out there the message I'm receiving
by December the scraps of leaves are left to scrape the sound of air
morning star into evening star
trekking from the Greek above the silver line
between the water & the land underscores Venus
tangled cordage our bread & fish
& where do the cards fall
item this tree on this hill alight in the world
invisible maps above the air corridors
high & silent aircraft float the silver air
googled & sweet alveolar consonants rubbing teeth in 'run' 'tap' 'Zeit'

into a touch into language into fractured slivers cracked one by one
I leave you from
a mirror's reflection
like hardcore cement sand
dredged from the estuary
the opposite of sweet spot
morning star into evening air

Wave

& what I didn't know was what
I was writing what I didn't know was
I was writing a sine wave I was
as Real as calligraphy as real as call
or watch as parcelled
I was left the real world was running in parallel to the virtual
as starlight to the star
& there the light is flying
water close to the wind a glass
a glance in the mirror a kickstart to memory tangled within this world
in weed patterns in transforms what the sky is written on & close
to the edge of the picture Life remote
as toys & as fetish
as maquettes dolls dummies
as mannequins to manufacture as human
is to facture real
as the claw crane grabbed
closed to touch the stuff
of stuffed toys mini candies
plastic dinosaur rigged as to skill
to spinning top to super bouncy ball
dumb memory of opposable thumbs
close in to touch as to the algorithm
as to the prize cheap as chance as trinket factored in
reality for the fee riddle me this rule of thumb
real as a wrecking ball & as seafront sirens

beyond grasp
there the clouds slip away beneath blue
there from this angle you are invisible
to these activist eyes the wrack line still breathing
where I left the message
or the message left me
palm upward see
the galaxy in my head I'm listening in
& these active eyes glass-smooth what gets close to the wind
a pebble sand grains milky glass next to
I left a message
I left what you should know
as if I left you
the weakest signals & seeing nothing the earth will forget us
like footmarks across the grass
water running
the house goes unfixed & I ate honey
there my mother fades as to blank
there there are gnats moaning or rain or meaning
dreamland at the end of the line

Night Poem

is to turn sunrise to profit
if they could what if
they did
word for word
the target the aim the god
& if he keeps saying it long enough for those to hear what they want
to hear the megaphone voice on repeat
to quack to sell the hooch out of the back
of the wagon huckster hustler
the softening tundra a skein of geese become a brace
fix for fix
on repeat to tedium given in to
& switch off

imagination despised this side of the moon
the end of signs & the end of things
the things that speak a certain truth
& the time to turn down the news
leaves flip somersaults over & over in the wind through the dust overleaf
read poems into the night
word to come over into breath
overheard words overhead
led into steam night air
passage to the star with its trailer tailing off
left as a sounding
left a blip or smudge on the monitor
flash dimmed over millennia
the dead rock of now
refuge for the refugee heart a star
arrested in amber
debris insect wing leaf-mould
bleep like a mother locked in memory locked in messages from afar
dull as a doll my coffin in my face

Peter Robinson

Ghost Photograph

Unsmiling, still, three figures stare
at the lens for a family photograph.
Round studio Liberty furniture
they're set on a rug of animal fur:
a father, his up-waxed moustaches,
the seated mother, her lazy eye,
and Norma, their blonde daughter
in sailor's suit, all posed before
the backcloth's painted hill-line…
See it emerge, preternaturally clear,
emanating from her mother's hair,
look now, an ectoplasmic smear,
like a flaw in the plate, a water stain,
another ancestor caught there…

The Last Lamps

'The time is out of joint …'
                    William Shakespeare

Between gnarled trunks down a parkland path
along beside the low embankment
are three wrought-iron standard lamps
still burning in broad daylight
as if they're out of sync or time.

There's sun diffused through clouds above them,
and the houses still weren't here
when Brunel built his railway earthwork.
The council placed these lamps, most likely,

for safety inside Palmer Park.
Their gleams among the arching branches
are like a gothic nave.

I'm steering clear of others by them
when, there and then, that glimpse arrives
in a time gone rotten before it's ripe,
our misread past, false future come
to exile us from our own lives.

from Blind Summits

Finally, the distancing pays us back in kind.
Whether it be with a low horizon,
piled clouds traversing big skies
or that optical illusion –

the water seeming vertical
with bands of brown and green
up to its sea-and-skyline.

*

The clouds at random altitudes
moving in diverse directions
are driven on as if competing
always to be somewhere else.

We're swerving as their shadows track us
north-north-west beyond the rows
of isolated bungalows.

Their Union Jacks and St George Crosses
underline the spaces opened
up before us and the losses
coming to that end.

*

Things picked from the vast expanses,
I'm better off down at sea level
amongst spots, flecks and spills of colour,

the white specks flocking in a tide-pool
or people on a strewn-out beach
observing social distances.
What fills the eye's beyond me.

*

With flies and wasp-like insects feeding,
cut adrift, a mussel farm post
is washed up on this shore.

Some of its empty shells, dislodged,
lie picked clean, ex-feasts-of-life
for the swooping seagulls.

*

Then even as life runs from the surf,
two kids with costumes on this shingle
take their tangled shadows with them.

The far dune-grasses bend away
in gusted breeze from farther south.
What fills the eye's beyond me.

Rosanna Licari

Finding Lucy, Ethiopia 1974

Asleep in the tent
Johanson's dream is a mix
of bone shards, psychedelic dust
and fragments of lyrics
from three-chord Beatles choruses
Yeah, yeah…
Hadar.
This place has to be full
of hominid bones.

Morning. A light breakfast.
The African sunlight is everywhere but
two hours on the stinking hot plain
reveals nothing. Johanson tells
the grad student, he wants to go back
to the small gully
that had already been checked
at least twice before. *Why not?*

In the dusty sediments
he finds a few horse teeth,
the skull fragment of an extinct pig,
antelope molars, some monkey jaw.
All in all, just bits. *Yeah…*
Nothing to sing about.

Midday and shirt sticks to skin,
sweat streams down Johanson's forehead,
his hat baking his brain
as the temperature heads
for 110° F. It's time to drive back
to a cold face cloth and lunch.
But as he turns to leave,

he sees something –
a broken ulna, an elbow part.
Yes! Yes! Yes!
And there is more.
Near this, a part of a small skull,
then a femur.
More walking, more bones:
vertebrae,
ribs,
pieces of jaw,
part of a pelvis – female? …
another bone
and another.
A hominid skeleton.
Could it be whole?

When it cools down,
all the fervid expedition will return,
carefully staking out the site
for digging and collection.

At camp, amid the night's banter,
laughter and endless whiskey,
the cassette player blares the Beatles'
"Lucy in the Sky with Diamonds".
We should call her that! someone says
and fossil AL 288-1 becomes "Lucy".
And she will bring light.

Hours and hours
of working on the bone jigsaw.
It's obvious weeks later.
No duplication.
It's one mother of a hominid.
Only one.
40% of a 3.2 million-year-old skeleton
that tells homo sapiens
that our ancestors walked
before getting a big brain.

Australopithecus afarensis:
Southern Ape from the Afar region.
The new species on the family tree.
The locals call her *Dinknesh,*
Amharic for "you are wonderful".
Love it… Love her…
Yeah, yeah, yeah…

Note: On 24th November 1974, Donald Johanson and Tom Gray found a hominid fossil that changed the understanding of the process of evolution.

The Vagaries of the Head: A Contemplation

1. Oculus

Consider the insect eye, a mass of hexagonal tubes forming a composite of the whole. Not unlike the seeds in the head of a sunflower. A plant that thrives in the full glare of light. All these forged by ancient code. Coiling strands that evolve life – a double helix etched with commands and functions. And code does weird stuff. Now imagine the Cambrian, the time when code branched off into two different evolutionary paths, one with backbones and one without, and on each developed the camera eye – a gelatinous core enclosed in a fibrous pot with an aperture that opens and shuts. Clear as a glass marble. Stare into the eyes of the cephalopods and admire our optics framed in a kindred way.

2. Auris

Long before ancient swimmers dripped onto land quivering in the offshore gust, the potential was there, behind the eye, the gill. Picture this developmental stretch forming a hole big enough for a middle ear in the fish head of *Panderichthys* – a transition between the creatures of fins and limbs, and a kissing cousin of an early tetrapod. This four-legged beast is pictured by an artist as almost pet-like, friendly, and bearing a sharp, toothy, late Devonian grin. From a studded collar, this relative might easily be tethered to a Bangalow palm to escape the steaming subtropical heat, as mp4 players move sound along ear canals, drumming membranes, vibrating strings of tiny bones while families of swim-suited bipeds, smeared with fake tan or sunscreen, eat hot chips and seafood, and dance by sparkling blue-tiled pools.

3. Nasus

Lean into your reflection, and journey as the evolving face. The rainforest sheltered you with large green leaves as ferns fanned the heat and sweat. You rubbed against buttress roots and became wider, flatter. The air, filled with the scent of sap, fuelled your journey into plenty: feathers slashed through the canopy full of bright screeching birds, the pythons moved slowly through the wet foliage and waited for them. Warm-blooded beasts sat on branches eating, grooming and you stalked them. Monkeys bared teeth, then fell when an arrow struck. You touched the flow of their iron-filled blood, inhaled its smell, flayed the hide from sticky flesh and sated, you slept. The northern lights pierced your dreams, deep voices called. Leaving the aroma of the dwindling forest, you tramped towards a star into a snow-strewn tundra. The receding light was veiled in autumn and hid in black winter. The spirits of water and ice came with the wind. Sculpted by them, you became long and narrow, breathed slowly to regulate your climate. In summer, the wildflowers burst into a world of sun that seemed to last for only a moment and you looked quietly at the strange, emerging creatures to get the measure of the kill.

4. Oris

A green deception. The minute hydra will rip open its mouth to feed then knit itself together effortlessly. There is value in the sting that paralyses floating prey above a lipless cavity. On land, mammalian evolution carved a cavity into the homo sapiens mouth – hinged, toothed, multi-purposed. A jaw crowned with teeth for tearing, cutting and chopping, then a backward prod to the crush and grind. A mouth that spits, blows hot or cold breath, tongues syllables with fleshy lips and air, and brings sound to a bilabial stop.

Janet Sutherland

Footnotes to Smalt Blue

"Observed that the rain on the previous night had been snow on the hills, those in the distance towards the frontier of Albania having their summits covered & contrasting very prettily with the smalt blue of the nearer ones"

George Davies 1847

To molten glass add cobalt oxide
for colour which is never strong—
if ground too fine the pigment weakens
so grind by hand and not for long

Old Stone Mountains

distance still lays down
complicated hues

    you might ask

if anything alters
is it us

    the question

our hidden
bones

    how did we get here?

layer on layer
utterly and completely blue

Loneliness

He wonders why the mountains look blue—
not until 1861 will it be clear
that complex equations govern the blueness

Until then it will seem that the mountains fade
like fabric worn for too many winters
like ink on paper which confines the heart

Land that is insubstantial in many torn layers
offers itself to the sky and seems to become it,
but when you arrive, is stony and problematic.

A scattering of light in molecules of air

Our eyes are more endeared to blue than violet
and blue is scattered almost as much as violet

when you look at mountains in the distance
blue light scatters inside the invisible

The Ortolan Bunting

Fragile bird of scrubland and field, weighing
less than an ounce in the hand. The song of
the male's like that of a yellowhammer,
the head, olive-grey, instead of bright yellow.

Size of a sparrow, but netted in flight;
caged up for weeks and fattened on millet,
gorging in darkness to double its weight,
then drowned in a vat, pickled in Armagnac.

Roasted eight minutes, and plucked for the table,
the feet go in first, one mouthful, one bird.

Molars come down, a wet crunch through the rib cage,
the whole thing at once.   Cover your head

out of pleasure or shame. A rush of hot fat scalds
the throat; slight bones prickle the roof of your mouth.
The yellowhammer's song from the tree is still just:
Chit, chit... ... little-bit-of-bread-and-no-cheese.

Kenny Knight

Sparrow

Take me back
to the wind
to that tree
spreading its shade
beneath the blue
watercolours of the sky

let me out
of this room
out of this cage
of lost feathers
out of this paint box
of congested art

take me back
back to my cluttered house
in the labyrinth of numbers.

Silver and Red

You open the door
come in out of the sun
close it and move deeper
into the house of scissors
the sky seen through the window
looks as white as your skirt
as blue as your eyes
which are hidden under a fringe
of brown hair which hangs
and drops over your shoulders.

I sit here facing the mirror
watching you run your fingers
thorough another man's hair
watching your lips move
sometimes without sound
or none that reaches me.
I think yet again
of the vanity of men
while waiting for you
to call my name
in that time I read a story
in the *Daily Mail*
which I quickly drop
back onto the table
as if my fingers
and my senses had been burned.

And then I see your lips move
and then my long hair
falls to the ground
summer has gone
and now its autumn
I know as the days
reach into October
that leaves will fall
all over the city
all over the land
but much sooner than that
someone else
some long-haired stranger
will sit where I sat
will take my place in the mirror.

And if I never see you again
what I'll remember most of all
will be your red fingernails
your smile in the mirror
and me stripped of language
smiling shyly back.

It Was Ducks Not Blackbirds
That Did It For Me

It was ducks
not daffodils
or five pound notes
that did it for me,
thunderstorms
in the teaching room
and a mad dash home
along Coombe Park Lane.
The streets were dry
and I remember crossing
three roads without looking
but there weren't
so many cars back then,
there were some
but not as many
as there were cats
in that book by T.S. Eliot
which I read some years later.
Cats lived out between the fields,
you could see their eyes at night
on the road to Modbury
or sitting on windowsills
looking wise and intellectual
like Egyptian professors.
Cats working undercover,
infiltrating our lives,
living rooms and sofas.

Out of breath
when I reached our house
I flung open the back door
looking for my mother
who stood alone
at the kitchen sink washing dishes.
She smiled and waved a greeting,

her hand a glove of soap bubbles
and in my eagerness to share
I slipped and skated over words
as if they were made of ice
my mind and my mouth
filled with images
of rain and feathers.
I had discovered something
old and beautiful.
It was ducks
not Dickinson
that did it for me.

Forgetting to wipe my feet
I stepped into the house
stepped onto the doormat
as if the doormat were a stage
a little bit of Lear
might have crossed.
Without any preamble
I grabbed a broomstick
making my debut
on the Plymouth Poetry Scene
to an audience consisting
of my mother and the family cat
and in the applause that didn't follow
I climbed the stairs
to the quiet of my room
where I looked out of the window
across the Tamar Valley
and in my imagination
sent an innocence of crows
flying north across the sky
towards Woodland Wood,
freewheeling across the years yet to come
before turning west
into the last of the day's blueness.

It was ducks
not Dylan
raindrops not rivers
that did it for me.
It was a ripple
of poetry on a pond,
a blink of blue eyes
gazing down into still water
it was nonsense verse
and nursery rhymes,
not Hilda or Ogden Nash
it was a seed which grew underground
into a tall and slender bush of marijuana
it was the year I hit seventeen
the year I got serious
about making language out of language
and sometime after that
I recall my mother saying
that there was more money
to be made robbing trains
than writing poetry
for Faber and Faber
and she was right
but I never wanted to rob
the midnight
train to Adlestrop,
never wanted to sell free verse
on the free market.
It was ducks
not dollars
that did it for me.

John Muckle

Recuerdos de la Alhambra

Unstoppably the river of love flows into a sea of harmony
& here below a man is listening to Andres Segovia
In the late twenties, a tripping canzonetta by Mendelssohn;
I imagine a boy listening to it on an old 78 rpm record
In Hampton, during the war, super-heterodyne radio valves
Buried in the back garden in order not to hear them shrieking.
Django Reinhardt's piercing vibrato, controlled passion
Restrained by intellect, attuned to a mathematics of pain.

A restless line encloses the boy's beautiful, absent mother.
She stares out into the road for hours, dreaming vacantly,
Mostly leaves her spouse to his varied & peculiar interests.
What does any of that rubbish matter to her? Nonetheless
She is a kind, loving mother to all of her four children.
Actually, she is the daughter of a famous music hall star.
The boy lies under the grand piano, transported to ecstasy.

He attends Hampton's school for unexceptional children
Where he meets my mother & sometimes pops around
To show off on her family's piano. Happy-go-lucky boy,
Proud of his talent & his grandmother's pub in Battersea
& after the war when Segovia comes again to Londres,
Julian & his father observe his technique with binoculars.
His right-hand particularly. How he does the light & feathery
The tremulous, choking lament of the gypsy peoples.
In memory of this my mother propelled me towards art.

North and South

North of here the towns recur, blossoming
Inkblots on moist blotting paper, flowering darkly
Suck up the whiteness, drinking it like water,
Which to their inhabitants is a sort of dry paper
Whose molecules spread out by capillary action, grim
Meanings then affixed to their dreadful names,
Bolted on like Bolton, cheating badly in Swindleton.
You'll know the kind of thing, most certainly.
It failed to stick last time, though names themselves
Sold well in US markets, climbing up glass sides,
Bulging a little in a vain effort at self-containment
To astonish for a moment before they burst,
Bathing the plains in a false-light, owl-light perhaps,
Mingled there with a few votive candles.

Usually commemorating a railroad magnate's
Daughter, which seemed to give American women ideas
Above their stations, under shaded canopies
Fanned out from drawing rooms to Fannin Street
To reemerge as great salon artists in great cities,
Dodging out of Dodge to master mechanical difficulties
While the Irish south emulated Richmond-upon-Thames,
Queens purloined Richmond Hill to the last letter;
Saginaw, Michigan paddled back to by exhausted canoeists
As folksingers shot rainbow fish in so many barrels.
Then the air cleared up & the sun shone through,
Turning out to be the name of the beast, apparently.

South of the river and the names commemorate
Mafeking and Bloemfontain, so many imperial battles
Spread thin in the memory of the present populace
And the right beer is no longer available to guarantee
Eternal life to its last lost consuming inhabitants.
I look for them through my telescope from where you are.
Why provide historians with the oxygen of publicity?
Let Winnie stand up proudly with Franklin D.

Although it was good to see the slaver Edward Colston
Tossed into the murky depths of Bristol Harbour.

Stating the obvious isn't good enough anymore.
We loved your noughts and crosses, give us more useful
Learning grids. Black Lives Matter, hand-lettered signs in windows
Proclaim it, and it's a pretty good feeling you get usually
On the way to the shops in your bo-leaf paper mask.
Why drag all what up again? Loofahs exfoliate dead skin.

Skateboarding

At the end of the avenue a boy does skateboard tricks
His phone propped up against a bollard
At the right angle to capture his solitary action.
Picking up thought off the pavement where
It has sometimes been rolled into the cracks
By winds that subsided a little earlier, I too will try again.
None of us were watching out for developments.
We thought jumping and flipping could theoretically
Go on forever. What can you do for your grandchildren
If what you had to pass on is beyond them?
They'll just have to learn how to do a normal life.
Perfecting tricks, they don't really matter a hoot
Unless somebody comes by with another board to flip.
I greet only admirers, study my reflection, listen
To the ticker. Bored by it all a thousand years ago
I thought it better not to tell you anything much.
Impossible but your memory still haunts me.
I'm planning one last gig. They'll flock into the death tent.
Let's face it, you never really took me seriously.

Peter Bakowski & Ken Bolton

Martin, Martin

"Who gave us these?"
"A woman from the Scout Hall," says Martin.
"Well," says Betty. Despairing.
She had meant the question rhetorically. "God knows
what they were thinking," she says, eyeing the books again:
                                        Modern
Business English; The Life of the Spider; Mark, the Match Boy;
Fables in Slang; Dave Dawson of the Air Corps; Penrod Jasper;
The Wit and Wisdom of Good Pope John; Boy Ranchers in the Desert;
A Mother's Prayer; Best Loved Poems of the American People; The Curse
of Darwin; Tom Sawyer; Crystal Vision (two copies); The Ordeal
of Harriet Marwood, Governess; Letters For All Occasions; A Heap o'
Livin'; A Pocket History of England; Ginger Meggs; Sergeant Silk,
the Prairie Scout; Adventures of Ulysses; The Southern Oscillation
Index; Gold Fools
                        —all in a box, wooden, with metal handles
on either side. Would once have had a lid.
"We could give them to the hospital," she says. "They sometimes
come down here asking for books." And *"What?"* she says to Martin—
who says, almost *sotto voce,* "Will they thank us?"—picking up the books
and taking them down the road. Not a lot of fun, Martin. Not
a lot of fun those books. Did the scouts *read* that stuff?

Hospital Stores

Woss-this-shit!? says Margaret bitterly—
amused and cocky, pleased to see Martin.
Martin wonders if Margaret is drunk already.
But she spins about confidently and puts things aside,
making room for the box, picks a book out
for a brief examination

and laughs. "Who reads this stuff?"
"My view entirely," says Martin, "Quiz nite tonight?"
he ventures, "—down at the *Four-Leaf?*" "Yeah, see you there, 6.30
maybe—for dinner first up." "Right. *Be* there."
"Oy?" *"I'll* be there. See you." Martin exits.
Margaret wheels on her good leg—her 'better' leg—
to peer after him—as he leaves the loading bay, out into
the daylight—her lips pursed as she calibrates
whatever it is—his mood, his height, his shirt.
Martin sometimes catches her watching him ("as if
shrewdly"—he has said to himself. Shrewd about what?)
The promise of the night is cheering, Margaret's touchiness though
taking off a little of the shine. But she likes his humour.

Back to Betty.

Meeting of Minds

Perez pushes out the front doors—when he finds them—
down the few steps, and out onto the street
and turns left and walks. Ten-thirty, eleven. No one about.
He is almost tempted to ask the girl, a schoolgirl,
what she is doing out and about and not in class—
but why should he? He laughs, looks up at the building
that has held him for more than two weeks.
It looks bleak, almost 'Soviet' to his imagination.
Built, he figures, some time in the seventies. Maybe earlier.
As a policeman he has known only its Emergency entrance.
This is what the larger whole looks like.

For her part, the schoolgirl—Chloe—is amused at
the small, stockily built man before her
who looks so much like her idea of a plain
clothes policeman. And she wonders if he is one. (No,
she thinks, on principle.) He is wearing a pale
mustard-yellow suit, white shirt, red tie (narrow),
has a dark moustache, a heart-shaped face—a look of impatience.

He gazes at her briefly and she feels she is 'clocked',
then discounted.

They pass each other—Chloe on to St Bridget's. Perez
walks a hundred feet—to a small, triangular park—
some trees, a round pond about a fountain—sits
and calls his wife.

Reading Matter

Veronika has come down to the bottom
                        of the hospital,
out the back—charged with bringing up some
fresh books for the television room, and
for some of the older women who particularly like to
                        read.

What is this woman's name, Margrethe or
                        something like that?

But the latter knows she's coming, and merely points—
to a box on a low table. Books.
Veronika selects a dozen. There are two copies
of one, so she puts one back. "Crap, that one,"
says the woman. "In fact they're all crap."
"In fact," she says with a delighted grin, "*books* are crap,"
and laughs. Veronika nods, chooses a few.
On the way up in the lift she glances at *Gold Fools*.
It looks relatively new. Immediately it feels
like one of the most tedious and exasperating books
she has ever read. She reformulates this to herself,
casting it in the interrogative—"*Was it,*"
she says to herself, "*one of the most exasperating books
Veronika had ever read?*" and laughs. She heads to the TV room.

Marta Saulnier

Marta Saulnier looks down, from a seventh floor balcony,
on elm trees and between them to the street and the broad sidewalks
that run either side: the long parade-like view
the hospital creates, stepped as it is, well back from the hue
and cry—the energy—of the street—the postcard-like sorts

of view that bring to mind the phrase *Champs-Élysées*.
No *Arc de Triomphe* at the further end—
but the pedestrians walk here with more space around them, an air
of elegance, Cartesian calm, of, almost, *Last Year
At Marienbad*. She sees her daughter's charming blend

of thoughtful schoolgirl and young adult poise—
that she will see soon now literally when Chloe will appear,
her upright posture, the broad hat and St Bridget's blue
uniform. She waters the plants, puts two plates, two
cups and their saucers out on the white iron table. Here

she will sit with Chloe and they will discuss their day,
have coffee and cake, or fruit. Later, a small meal,
before they will go out together to *Cul de Sac* or *Duck Soup*
or *Horse Feathers*, at their currently preferred small cinema. A burly man
    in a yellow suit,
had been about to accost Chloe this morning, then thought better of it. She'll

remind her: he had turned abruptly
and gone into the hospital. Chloe knows her mother's gaze
follows her for some moments each morning—but from such a height
it feels no invasion of privacy or *too much love*: like
the gaze with which she herself picks out Marta some days

thread her way between others, cross the park, to the library:
dusk, her mother's tailored grey suit and sometimes, even,
pill box hat that Chloe loves. "'The heroism,'" Chloe thinks,
"'of modern day life,'" its myriad stories—and of hers—which she thinks
will follow her mother's: law, librarianship, medicine?

A Parting of Ways

"They also gave us this," says Martin, wheeling in
a tea urn on a trolley. He lifts it and places it
before Betty. "Who did, Martin?" "Scout Hall," he says.
"Oh, this is much more useful." She considers it.
"We might almost keep it for ourselves," she says.
"Can we? Is it in our charter?" Martin wonders.
"Well who's going to check?" asks Betty.
"You don't look well, Martin," she examines him.
He would usually pursue his point, his objection—
though why was always the question, *why* would he?
Not today evidently.
"Big night," he said. He seemed to reel at the memory.
"Oh?" she said. "Quiz night," he elaborates. "Oh, yes—
with Margie, isn't it?" Martin is silent. A falling out.

Kerry Priest

The Carpet and the Dream Field

The Ogham Mother's Instruction Manual says you must picture it more like a handshake with a tree. First thought best thought. Take an interest in everything, Listen to music you don't like. Read books on boring subjects. Consider your transitions. Stay focused. Listen deep. Collect a twig from each tree in the Druidic tree calendar.

The wand-maker knows that the power source is not magician but tree. Baby has opened the box of cassettes, her two teeth inspecting corners. Awai-agadidi-meu-ba-ag-agg.

This alphabet is best approached by a deep encounter with each tree. Imagine how it tingles when sap juices flow, shivering towards a low sun. Wake up half an hour early to meditate. Wake up half an hour early to exercise. Wake up half an hour early to practice affirmations. Get more sleep.

The tape spool is seaweed on the blue carpet, amongst pirates and Vikings. A wand does not direct power so much as bestow it from the mother tree. The Portuguese man-o-war cassette has snagged a Gokstad Viking.

Picture it like a handshake with a tree, a moving of your mind slightly closer towards the realm of seeds and flecks, into an emptiness of wind. Take side routes. Allow distractions. Cultivate mistakes. Devise self-imposed limits. You are the story-teller making shadow puppet shapes on the cave wall. Give yourself a deadline. Be nice.

Baby gives her Mother an opalescent tape wig. Aaideeee-agawijadid-dididi. You will reach slowtime, sun-time, a constant shedding and returning.

Pinecone

Bach[1] kept a pinecone at his desk
to help with fugue mathematics,
but if I could amplify this wooden flower,
I'd invent a Plunk-Techno
born of the rasp of thumb on flake.

It reeks of the holy, a pew decoration
pinched from the Sagrada Familia.
A hundred gothic doors slightly ajar
suggest hello
but pinya won't admit a peek.

We're aerodynamic in the direction of earth
trapped in our wonder
raking fingers on brittle edges
counting fibonacci's petals – uno, uno –
held in a world of surface.

---

[1] The Bach flower remedy for distress and unhappiness following shock which can be timeless is Star of Bethlehem. Pine is the flower remedy for guilt and guilt is a subset of grief. Sweet chestnut liberates your mind from grief. Bach flower essences do not contain the plant itself, but dew collected in the morning when the sunlight has passed through them. Dr Bach intuited the healing powers of plants not through empirical testing, but through holding his hand near the plant and focusing on negative feelings. He thereby slowly uncovered a complex grid of layers of emotions spiralling around a core.

Julie Maclean

White witch hitching

Had I owned   a primrose 2CV
/two steam horses   four wheels/   in '73

I would not have   climbed into a truck
with that ugly farmhand   /pas Anglais/

who took country lanes   peut-être
to pluck the courage   to attack

swerving back   on the freeway   to the ferry
I missed   by fifteen minuits

Picked up by a suit   instead
in a slick sedan   dinner en famille

in a room out of   a Maupassant story
/autocorrecting to motor song, milk thistle, Newcastle/

Sailing the bay   next day Le Havre
in a couta boat   out of van Gogh's Saint Marie

How could I forget   the canvas-ripping
speed of jeune men   I was Jeanne d'Arc

Maid of Lorraine   /autocorrecting to
Dark Zen/   virgin soul intact

Back then   fearless   full of it
missing the flames   by an eyelash

Young

For G

'And so, being young and dipt in folly I fell in love with melancholy.'
            Romance, Edgar Allan Poe.

So, he says, you like my goth, do you? You know I like your goth. I've always told you I like your goth. He inhales seriously, wanting to know precisely what it is she likes about his goth. What is it about my goth you like? She doesn't want to have to spell it out—the way he dips his head into each cigarette, hauling smoke deep into his mystery. His rebel parka reeking of vampire. She doesn't think it cool to mention his black sheet hair slicing his heartbreak face, those vagrant eyes drooping ever so lightly, ever so lovely. She wants to keep it to herself—his blue winter lips, cloud breath, tender pity in back lanes, the agony of his dark beauty.

I like to think they did

on the other hand
a lifetime of not knowing
longing for the lost, the unattainable
is delicious, irresistible
Imagine the realized
a lifetime of co-habitation
with the known
knowing too well the same one

I confess my secret life
overflows with desire
for what will never be
I remember the words
I used   to be free
of my first love
casting him adrift
in the front seat of his
souped-up lime green car
I don't need you anymore
Quick escape in the dark

I needed a life
an alien time zone
in pursuit of the new
running from or to
Both   I'm sure
The thing is
I am forever in love
with the promise of him—
home-knits   crooked teeth
undying proclamations
first times
the blissful agony
in the perpetuity
of   *What if?*

Leviathan—ЛЕВИАФАН

the lie of the sea is changed   at a snail's pace   over this mammoth steppe
of bones, tusks, hide   erratics have arrived   in the form of belugas
whispering   one to another   *the lie of the land is changed*

but side by side   they cosy up   in the ease of old lovers
familiars split the sky   a gull   a bat   a singular crow
at the sink   the woman washes her hands   the lie of the sea is changed

out the window   on the move   this is not a story of love
hulls of dead boats   break the line of the sky   too late for an autopsy
a man in a beaten-up car   comes into view   across the bridge

smoking a cigarette   furiously   grey creeps over the folds
the lie of the land   is wrong   the woman washes her hands
makes tea   Russian Black   pirozhki stuffed with fungi

something has started to move   whales listen   the lie of the sea is wrong
wind whips it   into a frenzy   but thinly   the woman washes her hands
the man smokes furiously   over the bridge   narrow as a cervix

he pounds it like a madman   there are no flowers to be seen
the season for flowers   is gone   grey creeps over the folds
night birds run out of sky   the woman   washes her hands

clean of the man   the whales   bones of old hulls   she washes up clean
at the foot of the cliffs   a bag of soft rags   grey creeps over the folds
the lie of the land   is wrong   the man smokes furiously

Pagan Hardy Returns in lines
by Layli Long Soldier and Terry

This band of rainbow stone on road
drive behind the man and I am called the daughter
Foot not on the brake
Foot accelerating into wheat fields
Wheat   and I am the skipping daughter
Skipping skipping   pricked by ears and whiskers
I feel this now
          and you are the eyes of houses
Eyes saying keep your clothes on   on
Velvet curtains blue open to the vestry of St Mary's
cold pews, bee meadows
stinging nettles out the back
          Only I know this   And this
There was a deer   a butchered deer
among the epitaphs
its small hooves, blackberry eyes open to the girl
          Girl foraging for stories
in the long grass behind Saxon monolith
where roads become rivers
a swan and twin cygnets settle in the rush of a weir
Brass mills stand mum where lovers drown
          Know this
Pike and ram and plantain become the daughter
carrying her head as a ghost in the novel
on morning rides with Venn the reddleman

Red red man   Shut shut mouths of mummers

Ribbons of Morris dancers waving her away
across the waters

Daragh Breen

Birds in November

I Birds Wearing Bird Masks

A black rose blooms
suddenly and briefly
above the heavy fir tree
before the crows
appear to simultaneously
remove their masks
and disappear

the flower head remaining
only in the skull,
a lingering smell of smoke.

II Birds Against a Grey Background

Above a damp field
a ghosting of birds
against the low winter sky,
seen and then unseen,
tilting out of sight
before teasing themselves
back from some other world.

They have been flitting in
and out of existence
all morning,
silently returning
in dribs and drabs,
unwilling to stay too long
in this grey realm.

Waking
to the storm-felled tree
in the near corner of the next field,
the moon's shorn antler
the creature of it
having taken itself off to
some emptied industrial estate.
A brief throng of crows
hangs momentarily
in the memory of the tree
before they debris the rising wind.

Later
dusk is moths of sleet
dissolving against the window.

Lights in Mid-Winter

i Black Ash Park & Ride Car Park, Cork

In the dark of a
late December morning
the elevated car park lights
dim through the drizzle
with a feverish-ladybird glow

night's beetle had come
masquerading in its
Devil's Coach Horse guise
but dampness had fogged
its ballroom appeal.

The river, too full of life,
may have been giving them up all night,
winged creatures, casting them out
into the spill of the streetlights,
before pooling in darkness
beneath the bridge.

In December's still-dark
bridge traffic,
the upward V of its wings,
and a sudden stillness
before slipping down
the last foot or so,
like a Christ suddenly
having grown tired of
being crucified.

Haloes of headlights fail
to frame him
in his chosen dark.

Belinda Cooke

That Year

1

A Moment
For Mr Mullen and the Team

Each morning you spend
ever longer in the shower,
the plastic bead curtain
falls and falls....

You gaze down at these breasts
you'd always secretly despised
and realise, for the first time,
just how beautiful they are.

Never out, but now so much deeper in,
you love everyone and they love you,
you're introduced to the man
who will save your life (you love him to) —

when he pins you to the board
and sends you spinning,
you look him in the eye,
you do not flinch.

2

X marks the spot. Crescent moon.
Memento to this passionate affair.
God, perhaps, a step too far,
you start to believe in mountains.

See ludicrous me, gorgeous
in profile, see me in my
leopard skin pork pie hat!

I'm Chemo girl
in the Garden of Gethsemane —
O Christ!
Let this cup pass from me!

3

That Year

Then I could –

read again,
could walk again,

fatigue returned,
peaceful friendly luxury,
weak and rested and
looked after –

to be in a place where all
is done for you and love kicks back
satisfied, but to –

read again –
                    endlessly and focused –

to know it is three years.

This cannot have been me,
when nothing mattered,
not this absurd,
artist's – insane arrogance –
                    Ooo – look at me...
                         the channel to God...

No no – not that,
                but –
to read again,

having entered a secret club that knows
no fear, with our strange hats and hairdos
and our special handshakes…

But – 'You must grapple
with life you know',
that mess that is the world –
is to read again!

4

Rest

Morning wind. Morning wind.
I should be out there.
I should be perched on a
wet stone rock feeling the texture.
Not in here on this veggie day
only taking in the creaking,
the long kick back in the lazy boy chair.

Glitter of water.
Flexing made eye
in the wind.
Calls us.
Glints of emerald.
Turns to glass
with water and wind.

5

Twilight Walk

Out late though still bright
my mountain has all but disappeared
beneath a bland haze of grey mist
but what waves, what waves!

Who would think there could be such
a marvelous white, whistle of foam,
such crashing, nothing to what must
be happening on the coast proper.

Maria Stadnicka

Urban Afterlife

After a funeral, paperwork sits
in boxes at the end of desk rows.

Undertakers pause to change
suits before shift handover,

diesel engines flatten down
places of rest. Glass, iron, gravel.

Machines know: cities grow
in negative spaces, oil traces gift

buildings with signs of the cross.
Gliding hawks operate traffic

for clear passage. Night drops
its guard. Machines argue.

Power cuts add imagination
to people's lives. So much for

ending day's work seeking dawn.

Winter-Crossing

'It's a lot easier to stay alive in this world,
said the old woman, if everyone thinks you're dead.'
—Shalom Auslander

Before winter-crossing, I buy
appropriate clothing, change dress
to suit long-distance marches.

A last moment to empty my vanity case:
Travel light, it says in my antechamber.

I bite into *body-of-Christ* as if testing
gold in old coins. Mother always insisted:
Try everything at least once.

For unpredictable situations I write
on my palm an inventory of things
I am scared about:

places I travel to meet strangers,
colour, full stop's claw which follows
everything we forget to be for each other.

I fear befriending monsters and frost.
Past tense in statements about future.

Shoreline

At the funeral of a woman I know
I see her earlobes stripped off pearls.
Her temple rests on picture books,

still, monochrome like in old snapshots.
The graveyard's blues swirl
with greens. Water meets land
in seashells between her fingers.

Gales crush against the creases
of her dress and clouds dangle
off the church ceiling. I ask if she
has ever learnt to build a boat.

No. Never. What would I need it for?
She smiles from a distance
at the child I am breastfeeding.

Hierarchies

I inherit a house at the edge
of wild forests where I rarely go.

There will come a time when lost,
walking the back streets of memory

I check every gate for a way out.
Only one door handle fits my palm.

A found story I never thought
I was missing: home, a monument

that recognises my hand.
God forbid this mistake of certainty

for it brings familiarity of place,
it reduces everything to beginnings

until I admit that what is gone is taller
than me, louder, and always right.

Ask Jonah. He would say the same:
People see monuments as lessons of hierarchy.

They decide the order of things
according to confining walls.

The Mechanics of Pencils

(to Ai Wei Wei)

Six-thirty. A day growing mould
on corridors leading to shower blocks.
On foot in my room, I measure
space in back-and-forth steps.

Movements along tiled floors square
the symmetry between guards
and me. Seven-forty: bread time
then one hour of exercise.

Repetitive pacing during change
of guards. Their bones click in position.
The same place as yesterday.
Eleven. Daytime interrogation.

Ahead of compliance practice,
I write down my faults
with the mechanical rigour
of a loaded handgun. Exercise break.

Confined to my spot, I touch
imprisoned shades, crushed
to the size of my thoughts. Second round
of interrogations before five-pm dinner.

Hours with knife-edge creases trample
over my neck, carve my name
in words without vowels. Night cleans
my fingers and eyes off things

felt and seen during the day.
Next to my bed, soldiers on duty
check their watches. They, too, run
on the spot, bound to their movements.

Lydia Unsworth

Ranford (my things are in the garage)

furniture handed down
other people's choices
bedmates
the history of an object
I could sit in that living room and dance my eyes over all the collated strays
how a place
could come together
we made paneer in a sack
BBQed in the garage
sieved tomatoes, strained
the long side-drive of colour-coordinated recycling through raindrop slate
the click of a handle you force up a quarter-turn to secure
always so modern
and putting the right stick in the right hole
smashing the bottles
wheeling them to the gate
exams you can't fail
I made a three-course meal from a previous century
can't remember what it was but I remember I didn't ever want to eat it again
though I was glad I'd been transported

it couldn't last
we weren't all stayers
first one left the life the soul
then me after the strength of the various clusters
of Blu-Tac had all but ebbed away

because the thing I'd grown to own had since transformed
of course

I left
without moving out any of my things

a clutter of clothes in the shape of a body
half a cloud followed by three straight lines crudely sketched
by the open door

Kijkduin (a leap of faith)

there's a sea at my door
I drift in foam-space
walk out
as far as the current allows
and am pushed back again
like this
I gain my exercise
the outlines of a figure, a face
sprouts new kinds of flowers
I revert to the Latin
wearing thick gloves, thick socks
resting at traffic lights
I carry around with me a sack of life, adding new beans to the pile as I
         find them
I want everything in this sack and I want to enjoy it
the smallness of the space prevents
me from spreading out
I proliferate outside the house
in ways that are invisible
like this
I can manage
spinning down from the tree, flicking
up on the breeze
running my bare feet through the gushing water that cools the bridges
         on a hot day
there is a small raft on which I try to be gentle
the land as flat as our monthly fee
the pollen thick, the confetti blinding
on a hot day

A Field Remains

Perhaps you wouldn't call it a field, but at that time it hadn't quite morphed into anything else. It wasn't being 'used', though our childhoods were skimming through it. Those open spaces were erasures, and, like us, ill-defined. Grass stretched for miles, interrupted by fences, private land, electricity boxes, containers far from any kind of workplace. Blackberries and hyacinth balsam with their Parma Violet cloth-to-nose stink. We'd slip down ginnels behind rows of houses and this space that wasn't any longer where we lived but wasn't yet the motorway would open out. The motorway couldn't see us because it never was anywhere, was only ever a going, a driving-toward-death; and the adults, they didn't disobey the signage or peek over walls designed expressly to keep them out. Nothing for them to see but their imagination, all shaken out and creased. Wild fear, rumour, grey flowing capes half-seen and blinked away again. We lied and camped wherever it looked soft enough. Metal bridges, leftover streams, fat wet furniture, mossy and bright. We wanted rain in our shoes, we wanted to smell damp like the soil of the planet.

Cecilie Løveid

translated by Agnes Scott Langeland

Punishment

I am glad he received the punishment he got. As you know he will be led
up to every single grave.
He shall lay a basket with the past and a basket with
the present on each grave.
He shall wear dress uniform.
He will in addition have to empty the washing machine
for all the parents, do their sons' and daughters' chores.
Go to football practice, go to the gym, sing in the choirs;
he will be kept busy.
He shall record a lullaby
for every single one.
At the place where the roof collapsed onto the government desks in
        the Y-block,
he shall stand naked and lonely with his body smothered
in fragrant baby talcum.
He shall stand alone, a white screen will be pulled in front of him.
As you know he is condemned to look every single person in the eye,
and as you also know no-one will look him in the eye.
His bottomless pit of self-defence should be overturned.
Sudden, brave, unexpected questions should lay him bare.
He shall not be allowed to change his name. For wherever he goes,
someone will say his name. Someone will say his name and he
will turn round.
He will be the notorious penitent. He will have to carry out these tasks
alone, without the use of internet, manifestos, puppets, stand-ins or
lookalikes.
In the judgement laying out his sentence, it also states: None of these acts
of penitence must be photographed, sketched, cartooned or filmed.
No sound recording may be made, only the word *sorry* can be recorded.
You cannot go back and change what someone has endured.
For that reason, and even if he does all of this, it will be silent.

Fjordland

Jonas Dahlberg, *Memory Wound*, 2014. Land Art.

Jonas Dahlberg woke me up; I was asleep on the couch.
You must come here, he said.
Come and look out the living-room window! It is happening now all
    by itself!
It is a miracle, it just happened, right here in Hole.
The miracle too found it miraculous. Of course people, who had
    tried to say
that mountains cannot shout hooray or offer comfort, were also silent
    and astounded.
What happened, happened, for mountains can split in two after all.
Exactly when everyone had turned away, swivelled their chairs round,
    begun
to relax and were about to visit some town or other to hone their
    shopping skills
or to extend their patio, the tongue of land split in two.
The fjord poured in, as water cannot endure an empty void. But I saw
nothing. I was relaxing, had stopped looking out at the fjord. In that
    instant
the memorial was in place.
Exactly like the winning design. Only for real.
A sliced loaf of bread with a slice missing. Our own empty space with
water underneath, our empty space with sky above.
We must not tell anyone about this, Jonas Dahlberg; no-one will take
    us seriously, I said.
No, he said. No-one will believe that nature is like this, that it can
    comfort.
My daughter was furious and sad about my monument.
She feels so sorry for the whole of nature here, he said.

No, now this is beyond belief. It happened one evening. It
happened by itself. It happened in a parallel world.
It happened in a Fjordland, *the land that is not.*
I don't think you know what you are up to, Jonas, I said. I'll find
something for dinner. Would you like to watch the league match with
me? The micro went ping.

Comfort

They stood on the ferry there and back and wept on the ferry there
    and back.
Some stood on the fjord bed like reeds and some lay in the water, some
floated under the water, some lay on the path, some hid under
each other, some are dead, some are alive, some are bloodied,
some are broken, some stand on the ferry there and back; it will work
    out somehow.
But look: There is someone flying over the surface of the water.
It is Mrs Pepperpot who has wind in her sails. It is Pippi Longstocking
who is singing, it is Max and the Wild Things who are yelling and dancing,
it is Shaun the Sheep, who has a birthday, it is Babar the Elephant
who is on his way, he winds the film, there is Winnie the Pooh
who has a pot of honey, there is Mole, and Ratty
who has a boat and a red waistcoat,
although some of them are really a little too young
for this. No-one knows what will be concealed forever, and what
must be remembered and highlighted, and when there will be answers
to ordinary questions.
But they comfort as best they can, these angels.
They will be there forevermore on the ferry, there and back, there and
    back, when you
weep on the ferry, there and back.

Notes

Punishment
On 22 July 2011, Anders Behring Breivik, a young right-wing Norwegian
terrorist, planted a car bomb that killed eight government employees in the
Y-block and another government building in central Oslo. Later that day,
dressed in a police uniform, he shot and massacred sixty-nine young people
attending a summer camp, organized by the Norwegian Labour Party's
Youth Movement, on the island of Utøya, in Hole just outside Oslo. Prior
to carrying out these actions, he posted images of himself posing in military
dress uniform on the Internet and also laid out a manifesto. He received the
maximum prison sentence of 21 years, but with the possibility of extension as
long as he is considered a danger to society.

Fjordland

Clearly, 'Fjordland' refers to Norway, the land of the fjords. The island of Utøya lies in the Tyrifjord. However, *Fjordland* is also the brand name of a company that markets simple ready-made food. The products are promoted with idyllic images of pristine Norwegian countryside, cows in pasture, mountains and fjords, all of which present a dire contrast to the site of the massacre. Ironically, Breivik has complained that he has to eat such food in prison so this is an intended subtext.

The Swedish artist Jonas Dahlberg won the Norwegian government's memorial site competition to commemorate the Utøya massacre; his design involved splitting a narrow rocky peninsula in two. As the proposed site lay in the district of Hole near Utøya, several residents objected strongly to the design on the grounds that it would be a daily reminder of what they had experienced. The 'I' in the poem is a representative of the local residents who contested the construction of Dahlberg's winning design. The decision to construct Dahlberg's memorial was revoked after a court case. A different monument on the mainland is now under construction to be unveiled on the 10th commemoration on 11 July 2021. An illustration of Dahlberg's design is on the web pages of *The New Yorker*: https://www.newyorker.com/tag/anders-behring-breivik

Hole is the name of the rural council area where Utøya is situated.

Comfort

A ferry transported the young people, mainly teenagers, out to the summer camp on Utøya. After the massacre they were found dead and injured all over the island and in the water.

I have altered most of the names of the characters from the original ones in Norwegian children's books, to ones that are more familiar to English readers (but also known to Norwegian children from TV and books). For example, 'Labbetuss', who is a popular figure in a children's TV programme in Norway, is changed to 'Shaun the Sheep', which is also broadcast on Norwegian television. All these characters have given the teenagers pleasure when they were children.

Gérard de Nerval

translated by Ian Brinton & Michael Grant

Disinherited

I am the shadowed one – the one bereaved– the unconsoled,
The Prince of Aquitaine within the ruined tower:
My one and only *star* is dead, – and my constellated lute
Is burdened with the black *sun* of *Melancholia*.

In the darkness of the tomb, you who have consoled me,
Bring back here to me Posillipo and the sea of Italy,
The *columbine* so greatly pleasing to my desolated heart,
And the trellis where both vine and rose are one.

Am I Love or Phoebus?... Lusignan or Biron?
My forehead is stained red from the kisses of the queen;
I have been dreaming in the grotto where the siren swims...

And I have twice in triumph crossed the Acheron:
Playing turn by turn on Orpheus' lyre
The sighs of the saint and lamentations of the fay.

Golden Verses

Now then! Everything is sentient (Pythagoras)

Free-thinking Man, do you believe you are alone a thinker
In this world where life transfigures all there is?
Forces you possess dispose your freedom,
But the universe is far removed from your reflections.

Respect the living soul in every creature:
Each flower is a blossoming of Nature:
A mystery of love rests in metal:
'Everything is sentient!' And it holds you in its power.

Beware the gaze the blind wall turns on you!
Even words are tied to matter . . .
Do not make it serve an impious purpose!

A hidden God often dwells in dark corners:
And like an eye born covered by an eyelid,
A pure spirit quickens beneath a crust of stones!

Anteros

You ask me why my heart brims with rage
And though my neck is pliant my head remains unbowed;
Descended from Antaeus and his race,
I hurl the spears back against a conquering god . . .

Yes, I am one of those the Vengeful God inspires,
He has placed his angry kiss upon my brow,
Under Abel's sallow skin, alas! I am stained
Time after time by the bloody and relentless mark of Cain.

Jehovah! The last, cast down by your genius,
Who, from the pit of hell, cried out "O tyranny!"
Was my forebear Baal or my father Dagon . . .

They plunged me thrice in the streams of Cocytus,
Now alone I guard my mother the Amalekite,
I sow the ancient dragon's teeth before her feet again.

Artemis

It strikes thirteen again... She is, as ever, first;
And, as ever, on her own – or it is the only moment;
For you, O are you queen, the first or last?
Or are you king, the only or final lover?...

Love whoever's loved you from the crib to casket;
She I loved alone loves me still in tenderness;
She is death – or the dead one... O delight! O torment!
The flower she clutches is the *hollyhock*.

Saint of Naples, grasping fires in your hand.
Rose of violet heart, flower of Saint Gudule,
Have you found your cross in the wasteland of the skies?

Down, white roses, down! You are an insult to our gods,
Down with you, white phantoms, from your burning heaven:
– The saint of the abyss is more sacred to my eyes!

Ivan Štrpka

translated by James Sutherland-Smith

from Bebé: One Crisis (*Bebé: jedna kriza, 2011*)

I.

Your gaze

Your gaze feels like a sharp knife. My gaze feels like a sharp knife: Bebé. Snail mouth, naked silence. Everything is naked, my dear. A relationship outside speech. Unspeech. A relationship and unspeech. A relationship like unspeech? Unspeech like a relationship? And Bebé.

***

A gaze is holistic or not at all, anima mea. Or it falls completely apart. And where are the words? Where is the language?
We run through large empty stations without trains and without people: a rumble heaves up from the marble paving, a pounding arises: another body in another body, another body in another body, another body in another body. Up to an explosion: Bebé!
Are we conspirators in this? Allies?

***

Or in cinemas? The film tears. Water flows. The film jams. The film sticks to us. In a single glance.

***

At first glance:
Blood is hidden deep in the fleece, in which voices return to their bodies. And what I see is a coin, a naked coin: smooth and empty on all possible sides.

II.

For Bebé

Utterly wipe away every trace in the sand.
Cast your smile at the smoky pavement,
vanishing train and mute scapegoat,
who are always dawdling behind us.

You, who in the bowels of sleepless nights
absently circle a sticky silence
in the depths of sleep a slowed
taxi and stick of dynamite, over and over

lightly tinted by the intact enamel
of teeth in your scarlet mouth,
at every corner you take from the city

solid ground under your feet. Bite through the days!
You, who've from daybreak burn all the phonemes before you
and all the bridges to their innumerable archives.

On Bebé's smooth skin

This is a light sketch
Of your procedure: follow the blade. Without moving
sit further to the edge, fundamentally
your back to every wet map that
has just overflowed. Only unintentionally,
without punctuation. On smooth skin
just beyond the edge of a shriek.

Finally, Bebé

Finally, the victim must be untouched. Entirely,
as intact as Your skin, which doesn't tolerate
a scratch, tattoo or even the most delicate
cut. It clings to you so completely that

you yourself don't stray on to its dazzling surface.
You won't transgress and vituperate. It's just you, just you
swim in it. Without connection. Never
do you cover a network.

Bebé, stop!

You who emptily
move your lips, Bebé!
Keeping silent as You always indicate
thus a little satiated with dumb lamb.
The lamb is always there. The lamb is always thus a little.
thus a little beyond. The lamb is always
a little soft shadow grazing
outside it. Your own thirst. The lamb is
a creature outside language. A shape outside speech. A little
naked, ready for anything. Thus always a little bit
with one leg outside its own fleece
it crosses the network easily.
Bebé, stop it ! Stop! Oh, stop it,
anima mea! Blood colours! Hunger
can't be eaten.

Bebé calls

Bebé sits motionless in the scorching sun on the stone of the step.
Mobile phones persist trilling in abandoned beds, in empty houses, on
corners, on quietened playgrounds, in motionless cars, in dresses, in
measured hands almost blazing from the sun.
A glittering, transparent fish slowly penetrates inside her head, from ear
to ear connecting a whole mute boundlessness.
Bebé is silent in her alabaster skin. It's a naked act: a call in an empty
network that automatically multiplies its own emptiness: it produces
echoes not preceded by a voice.
Bebé glows. Water glosses.
Silence *pisses* it. From word to word.

Fleeting Portrait of Bebé

To direct means to aim, to move towards something. To somewhere. Actually, not to stand still. Not even in front of a mirror, dear Bebé. To direct means to watch and wait, not to shatter. To direct means to step out of the circle.

***

To direct into the mirror means heading up against a gale. Into a diamond interior, into a silent storm in a golden eye.

***

You walk against an empty gale, Bebé. Against the current of a mirror, in which you will never find yourself. What is it you're meeting there? Everywhere only white clumps and snippets of falling quiet on which you sparkle.

***

Growing white floes of crumpled paper slowly drift along the land surface overflown by the sun and shadow: all those reflections and references trembling by You.

***

Standing you shove off with a long, thin pole from an obscure depth, in a motionless, narrow, wobbly boat in the middle of a smooth surface. Even the breeze has stopped. You mirror yourself wholly in the vanishing circle of that uncertain shove.
Bebé, you reflect the mirror.

***

You mirror and multiply. Exactly the same. A short process: Bebé meets Bebé fleetingly in the midst of fleeting gestures. Bebé the Second listens absently for a long time and silently passes on her secrets to Bebé the

Third. She hesitates a while before she throws a stone on the surface, before she accuses you. And Bebé the Fourth, the one with the split face, in gold, without hair, or even eyelashes, will condemn you without batting an eye.

***

The mirror indicates. The blank paper in front of Your face quietly flares and slowly begins to submerge.
Pure silent fury smoulders in your clairvoyance.

III

Bebé is now

Bebé is outside speech. It's an aquatic life. Off firm ground. Bebé is now a stationary surface outside the topography of flatlands, love's bolt from the blue and tamped down routes.
Bebé only accepts, reflects and mirrors: Bebé's slow acts. Bebé is a clean, inaccessible exterior, a surface freezing without the slightest movement. In vain I lure. In vain I submerge my naked elbow and my whole forearm. The transparent armour strengthens. The fish can't be caught. The ice is growing. Muffled it cracks underfoot. Thin smoke rises from the wintering grounds of phonetics, from the seats of silent fishermen. Every smile has frozen here.
I only take away the translucent shadow of an uncaught fish lagging closely behind my blackening hand. Just the crackle of ice without a single syllable and its slight variations at the back. Just the bare record of the word SILENCE in my head. Only the bare mirroring of a place without phoneme and without firmness under a stationary surface. A freezing echo of Your hair and a Tower of verbal bones, Bebé!

Notes on Contributors

TOMI ADEGBAYIBI is a Nigerian poet from London. She has self-published a small collection, *DSM-? A Poetic Revision* (2018). Her poems have appeared in publications such as *Datableed*. Current projects are concerned with moving around the world, how our senses navigate and inform these movements and how these issues might be made to fit into poetry.

PETER BAKOWSKI is a Melbourne poet & **KEN BOLTON** lives in Adelaide: they collaborated on this series of 'glimpses', or 'moments', over the last year or so. The project will appear as *Nearly Lunch*, from Wakefield Press, Adelaide—which also published their similar *Elsewhere Variations*.

DARAGH BREEN has two collections from Shearsman Books, *What the Wolf Heard*, and most recently, *Nostoc* (2020). He lives in County Cork, Ireland.

IAN BRINTON has edited two collections of essays on J. H. Prynne, and another on Peter Hughes, for Shearsman Books. He has translated Mallarmé (*Poems*, Muscaliet Press), Valéry and Bonnefoy with Michael Grant, and Baudelaire on his own (*Paris Scenes*, Two Rivers Press).

BELINDA COOKE's translations include Kulager Ilias Jansugurov (Kazakh N.T.A., 2018); *Forms of Exile: Poems of Marina Tsvetaeva* (The High Window Press, 2019); *Contemporary Kazakh Poetry* (C.U.P, 2019). Her own poetry includes *Stem* (The High Window Press, 2019) and *Days of the Shorthanded Shovelists* (forthcoming from Salmon Poetry). She is currently working on a full memoir of her mother's life.

STUART COOKE's latest books include the poetry collection *Lyre* (University of Western Australia Press, 2019) and a translation of Gianni Siccardi's *The Blackbird* (Vagabond, 2018). He lives in Brisbane, where he lectures in creative writing and literary studies at Griffith University.

GARETH CULSHAW lives in Wales. He has two collections from FutureCycle called *The Miner* and *A Bard's View*. He is a current student at Manchester Met.

CARRIE ETTER is Reader in Creative Writing at Bath Spa University, and is the author of four full-length collections, the most recent of which is *The Weather in Normal* (Seren, and Station Hill Press in the USA, 2018).

GERRIE FELLOWS has two titles with Shearsman Books, the most recent being *Uncommon Place*. A Scottish writer, with roots in New Zealand, her poetry appears in many anthologies of Scottish writing.

MICHAEL GRANT has edited a number of prose works including *T.S. Eliot: The Critical Heritage*, *The Modern Fantastic* and *The Raymond Tallis Reader*. His most recent works of poetry are *The First Dream* (Perdika Press) and *The White Theatre* (vErIsImIllItUdE).

MARIA JASTRZĘBSKA's most recent collection was *The True Story of Cowboy Hat and Ingénue* (Cinnamon Press, 2018). She has co-edited various anthologies including

Queer in Brighton (New Writing South, 2014) and translated Justyna Bargielska's *The Great Plan B* (Smokestack, 2017).

KENNY KNIGHT lives in Plymouth, where he runs CrossCountry Writers. He has two collections from Shearsman Books, *The Honicknowle Book of the Dead* (2009) and *A Long Weekend on the Sofa* (2016).

AGNES SCOTT LANGELAND was born in Scotland but lives in Kristiansand, Norway. She retired from teaching at the University of Agder in 2015 and has continued to translate works by several contemporary Norwegian writers. Her translation of Stein Mehren's verse, *To the Outermost Stars*, was published by Arc Publications (2019).

ROSANNA LICARI's work has appeared in a number of Australian and international journals. She recently won the 2021 American Association of Australasian Literary Studies Poetry Prize, and teaches English to migrants and refugees in Brisbane.

FRAN LOCK is a sometime itinerant dog whisperer, the author of numerous chapbooks and seven poetry collections, most recently *Contains Mild Peril* (Out-Spoken Press, 2019). Her eighth collection *Hyena!* is due from PB Press later this year. She is an Associate Editor at *Culture Matters*.

CECILIE LØVEID is a Norwegian poet, dramatist and novelist from Bergen. She has published eight collections of poetry. For her most recent, *Vandreutstillinger*, ('Exhibition Catalogues', Oslo: Kolon, 2017), she was awarded two prestigious prizes. Her latest collection, *Piggeple* ('Thorn Apple') is expected later this year from Kolon.

JULIE MACLEAN has published four pamphlets and one full collection. *When I Saw Jimi* was shortlisted for the Crashaw Prize (Salt Publishing) and was joint winner of the Geoff Stevens Memorial Poetry Prize (Indigo Dreams, 2013). She lives in Australia. www.juliemacleanwriter.com

FOKKINA MCDONNELL has two collections, *Another life* (Oversteps Books, 2016) and *Nothing serious, nothing dangerous* (Indigo Dreams Publishing, 2019), and the pamphlet *A Stolen Hour* (Grey Hen Press, 2020). In 2020 she received a Northern Writers' Award from New Writing North for *Remembering / Disease*. Broken Sleep Books will publish the collection in late 2022.

JOHN MUCKLE is a fiction writer, poet and critic. His many publications include the novel *Falling Through* (2017), and a poetry collection, *Mirrorball* (2018), both from Shearsman Books. He lives in North London, and works as a teacher.

SIMON PERCHIK is a retired attorney whose poems have appeared in *Partisan Review, Forge, Poetry, Osiris, The New Yorker* and elsewhere. His most recent collection is *The Family of Man Poems* published by Cholla Needles Arts & Literary Library, 2021. For more information see his website at simonperchik.com

KERRY PRIEST's debut pamphlet, *The Bone Staircase* is out with Live Canon in 2020. She has been published by *Acumen, Dark Mountain, Emma Press and Poetry Salzburg Review*. She was one of Eyewear's Best New British and Irish Poets 2018. Her experimental poetry sound pieces have been played on BBC Radio 3.

PETER ROBINSON's 2020 publications were a sequence of poems, *Bonjour Mr*

Inshaw (Two Rivers Press), and *Poetry & Money: A Speculation* (Liverpool University Press). *The Personal Art: Essays, Reviews & Memoirs* is due from Shearsman Books in Autumn 2021 as is *Peter Robinson: A Portrait of his Work* edited by Tom Phillips.

PAUL ROSSITER lives in Tokyo, where he runs Isobar Press, specialising in English-language poetry from Japan and translations of Japanese modernist and contemporary poetry. His own most recent book, which includes the poems printed in this issue, is *The Pleasures of Peace* (Isobar Press, 2021).

SIMON SMITH is a poet who lives in London. His most recent books appeared in 2018: *The Books of Catullus* (Carcanet Press), *Day In Day Out* (Parlor Press) and *Some Municipal Love Poems* (Muscaliet Press). The poems in this issue are from a new sequence of poems called 'The Magic Lantern Slides'. He is presently also translating a selection of poems by Du Fu.

MARIA STADNICKA is a writer, journalist and Ph.D researcher at University of the West of England, Bristol. Her research explores socio-cultural trauma transmission, personhood and collective memory. She is the author of *Buried Gods Metal Prophets* (2021), *Somnia* (2020), *The Geometric Kingdom* (2020), *The Unmoving* (2018) and *Imperfect* (2017). Further information about her work, collaborations, and reviews at www.mariastadnicka.com.

IVAN ŠTRPKA grew up in southern Slovakia. In 1963–1969 he studied Slovak and Spanish at Comenius University in Bratislava. Štrpka entered literature as a member of *Osamelí bežci* (The Lonely Runners), a triumvirate of poets including himself, the late Ivan Laučík and Peter Repka. After 1968 he and the other Lonely Runners were not allowed to publish their work and he made a living as a dramaturge and by writing song lyrics, especially for the Slovak rock legend, Dežo Ursiny (1947–1995). By the mid-eighties, he became the editor in chief of the magazine *Mladé rozlety* and then the editor in chief of the newly established literary weekly, *Literárny týždenník*. From 1990 to 1993, he was the editor in chief of the weekly *Kultúrny život* and then in 1999 he became the editor in chief of the literary magazine *Romboid* until 2010. Books of his selected poems have been published in numerous languages including Arabic, Bulgarian, French, German, Hungarian, Italian, Polish and Spanish.

JANET SUTHERLAND has four collections from Shearsman Books, the most recent of which is *Home Farm* (2019).

JAMES SUTHERLAND-SMITH was born in Scotland in 1948, but lives in Slovakia. He has published seven collections of his own poetry, including *The River and the Black Cat* (Shearsman Books, 2018). He has translated a number of Slovak poets, the most recent being is Mila Haugová: *Eternal Traffic* (Arc Publications).

LYDIA UNSWORTH's latest pamphlet *YIELD* (KFS Press) and novel *Distant Hills* were released in 2020. Her new collection *Mortar* was published by Osmosis Press in 2021. Recent work can be found in *Interpreter's House, Bath Magg* and *Blackbox Manifold*. Twitter: @lydiowanie

CLIFF YATES's recent poetry collections are *Jam* (Smith/Doorstop, 2016) and the pamphlets *Birmingham Canal Navigation* (Knives, Forks and Spoons, 2020) and *Another Last Word* (Red Ceilings Press, 2021).

SHEARSMAN
129 & 130

WINTER 2021 / 2022

GUEST EDITOR 129 / 130
KELVIN CORCORAN

GENERAL EDITOR
TONY FRAZER

Shearsman magazine is published in the United Kingdom by
Shearsman Books Ltd
P.O. Box 4239
Swindon   SN3 9FL

Registered office: 30–31 St James Place, Mangotsfield, Bristol BS16 9JB
(this address not for correspondence)

www. shearsman.com

ISBN 978-1-84861-773-5
ISSN 0260-8049

Subscriptions and single copies

Current subscriptions – covering two double-issues, each around 100 pages in length – cost £17 for delivery to UK addresses, £23 for the rest of Europe (including the Republic of Ireland – although we are no longer selling into the EU, apart from Ireland), £25 for Asia & North America, and £28 for Australia, New Zealand and Singapore. Longer subscriptions may be had for a pro-rata higher payment. Purchasers in North America and Australia will find that buying single copies from online retailers in there will be cheaper than subscribing, especially since the recent drastic price-rises for mail to the USA and the Antipodes. This is because copies of the magazine are printed in there to meet orders from local online retailers, and thus avoid the transatlantic mail.

Back issues from nº 63 onwards (uniform with this issue) cost £9.95 / $17 through retail outlets. Single copies can be ordered for £9.95 direct from the press, post-free within the U.K., through the Shearsman Books online store, or from bookshops. Issues of the previous pamphlet-style version of the magazine, from nº 1 to nº 62, may be had for £3 each, direct from the press, where copies are still available, but contact us for a quote for a full, or partial, run.

Submissions

Shearsman operates a submissions-window system, whereby submissions may only be made during the months of March and September, when selections are made for the October and April issues, respectively. Submissions may be sent by mail or email, but email attachments are only accepted in PDF form. We aim to respond within 3 months of the window's closure, i.e. all who submit *should* hear by the end of June or December, although we do sometimes take a little longer.

This issue has been set in Arno Pro, with titling in Argumentum.
The flyleaf is set in Trend Sans.

Contents